Joh___ _t - Kemp

GROUP COMMUNICATION

Prentice-Hall Series in Speech Communication
Larry L. Barker and Robert J. Kibler, Consulting Editors

ARGUMENT: AN ALTERNATIVE TO VIOLENCE
Abne Eisenberg and Joseph Ilardo

ARGUMENTATION: INQUIRY AND ADVOCACY
George W. Ziegelmueller and Charles A. Dause

BEYOND WORDS
Randall Harrison

COMMUNICATION: CONCEPTS AND PROCESSES
Joseph A. DeVito

COMMUNICATION VIBRATIONS
Larry L. Barker

DESIGNS FOR PERSUASIVE COMMUNICATION
Otto Lerbinger

GROUP COMMUNICATION: DISCUSSION
PROCESSES AND APPLICATIONS
Alvin A. Goldberg and Carl E. Larson

LANGUAGE: CONCEPTS AND PROCESSES
Joseph A. DeVito

MASS NEWS: PRACTICES, CONTROVERSIES, AND ALTERNATIVES
David J. LeRoy and Christopher H. Sterling

MONOLOGUE TO DIALOGUE: AN EXPLORATION OF
INTERPERSONAL COMMUNICATION
Charles T. Brown and Paul W. Keller

ORGANIZING A SPEECH: A PROGRAMMED GUIDE
Judy L. Haynes

PERSPECTIVES ON COMMUNICATION IN SOCIAL CONFLICT
Gerald R. Miller and Herbert W. Simons

PERSUASION: COMMUNICATION AND INTERPERSONAL RELATIONS
Raymond S. Ross

THE PROSPECT OF RHETORIC
Lloyd F. Bitzer and Edwin Black

SPEECH COMMUNICATION: FUNDMENTALS AND
PRACTICE, third edition
Raymond S. Ross

TRANSRACIAL COMMUNICATION
Arthur L. Smith

GROUP COMMUNICATION

discussion processes

and

applications

ALVIN A. GOLDBERG
University of Denver

CARL E. LARSON
University of Denver

Prentice-Hall, Inc., Englewood Cliffs, New Jersey

Library of Congress Cataloging in Publication Data

GOLDBERG, ALVIN A.
  Group communication: discussion processes and
applications.

  Includes bibliographical references.
  1. Communication.   I. Larson, Carl E., joint
author.   II. Title.
P91.G58   301.14   74–5295
ISBN: 0–13–365221–1

Printed in the United States of America

10   9   8   7   6   5   4   3   2   1

PRENTICE-HALL INTERNATIONAL, INC., LONDON
PRENTICE-HALL OF AUSTRALIA, PTY., SYDNEY
PRENTICE-HALL OF CANADA, LTD., TORONTO
PRENTICE-HALL OF INDIA PRIVATE LIMITED, NEW DELHI
PRENTICE-HALL OF JAPAN, INC., TOKYO

To Judy and Georgie

contents

understanding group communication

The Nature of Group Communication, 3

toward effective group communication

II

Experiencing Group Communication, 161

preface

With the publication in 1939 of the first edition of *Discussion in Human Affairs* by James H. McBurney and Kenneth G. Hance, discussion became firmly established as an important area of teaching and scholarship in speech communication. McBurney and Hance, along with most dicussion specialists of that period, were concerned primarily with formal discussion—that is, with group interaction that took place in relatively formal public or private settings and that focused on significant tasks or problems. Early discussion specialists usually ignored the process or psychological aspects of discussion. It was not until discussion texts and courses began to include units on process that the phrase "group communication" appeared as an occasional alternative to the "discussion" label.

Until recently, a primary purpose of discussion texts and courses was to train better discussants. Discussion was viewed largely as an art rather than a science. Emphasis, generally, was on prescription rather than description. An understanding of the discussion process was important not for its own sake but because it enhanced performance. During recent years there has been a modification in this pattern. Along with the growing emphasis on scientific approaches to many specialties in the speech communication discipline, discussion, or group communication, is on its way toward becoming an area of scientific study, as well as an area of skill training and performance. This change, as well as the other changes and developments that have occurred over the years in the group communication area, can be attributed in part to the influence of a number of important traditions.

In the introduction to their discussion text, *The Dynamics of Discussion* (1960), Dean C. Barnlund and Franklyn S. Haiman identify two different traditions that have influenced the field of group communication. Supporters of one tradition saw group discussion as a basic methodology of democracy. They felt that through small-group discussions, citizens in a mass society could participate overtly rather than vicariously in the making of decisions that affect them. The leaders of this tradition wrote books about discussion and supported community discussion groups, college courses in discussion, and similar developments. In a sense, this group saw group communication as a vehicle for generating and expressing an interest and involvement in civic affairs; such skills as clear thinking, problem solving, and decision making were stressed.

The second tradition that has influenced the discussion area, according to Barnlund and Haiman, is psychological in its focus. It is generally associated with the group dynamics movement and with the work of psychotherapists, organizational theorists, and behavioral scientists. The writings and applications of this second group have focused on self-insight, awareness of others, and on the understanding of group process. The members of this second tradition are also very much concerned with democracy, but they are less interested in civic involvement and the discussion of important issues than they are in the values of democracy such as cooperation and a concern for others.

Both traditions identified by Barnlund and Haiman have influenced the present text. The tradition that has focused on civic involvement and the effective handling of ideas contributed greatly to our understanding of the task aspects of group communication. The tradition that has emphasized the psychological or social-emotional aspects of discussion enhanced our insight into the process aspects of group communication. However, the present text has been strongly influenced by a third tradition as well. It is the tradition of empiricism in speech communication already alluded to in this preface—the effort throughout the years to establish speech communication as an area of scientific study and research.

Speech communication can be viewed as a derivative discipline concerned with skill training. but the empiricists have demonstrated that it is more than an area of application or artistic performance. Charles H. Woolbert, Howard Gilkinson, Franklin Knower, and Elwood Murray are some of the pioneers who helped establish and sustain the empirical tradition in speech communication during the first half of this century. More recently, the group of scholars associated with the

1968 New Orleans Conference on Research and Instructional Development in Speech Communication, and many others, have maintained the tradition and given it new vigor and thrust.

In the area of discussion or group communication, the empirical tradition does not represent a rejection of the other two traditions described by Barnlund and Haiman. Instead, it enhances the developments in group communication that are associated with the rhetorical and the social-psychological traditions by adding a new emphasis on inquiry—inquiry designed not just to discover ways to improve the effectiveness of discussion groups, but inquiry engaged in to better understand the group communication process itself.

It has been noted that, typically, books on discussion or group communication have been concerned with how to be a better discussant or group leader. Even those chapters or sections supposedly devoted to a description and analysis of the discussion process generally have dealt not with group communication as it actually occurs, but with group communication as it ideally ought to be. This prescriptive, idealized focus has been a deliberate one on the part of textbook writers and teachers of discussion, for their goal has traditionally been to develop the discussion skills of their readers and students and to improve the quality of discussion. Textbooks and course content were means to these ends, not ends in themselves.

Speech communication, it has been pointed out, is becoming more of a scientific discipline with a content designed to provide systematic insight into basic communication processes, not just insight into how to behave more effectively in speech situations. This latter goal should not be minimized. It is after all, the raison d'être of the speech profession. No other academic discipline is devoted so explicitly to the practical implications of study and research in communication. There is an obvious need, however, for speech scholars themselves to conduct some of the basic communication study and research that they draw upon to develop principles of good performance if they wish to be more than practitioners or trainers. It is clear to most contemporary speech communication teachers and scholars that their respectability is related to their ability to make significant basic contributions to the communication literature instead of relying too heavily on the contributions of others.

There is another and perhaps more vital reason for emphasizing description rather than prescription. It seems reasonable to believe that significant improvement in communication performance that is more than just superficial and temporary occurs not because the learner has received good advice, but because he has a better understanding of the communication process. This is not to suggest that intellectual learning is sufficient to bring about a change in an individual's skill as a communicator. We can all cite examples of athletic coaches who have a good understanding of games that they themselves play rather poorly, or of experts in human relations who have trouble getting along with their neighbors. Nevertheless, intellectual insight plus opportunities to practice relevant communication skills may be as effective in improving performance as practice that is merely coupled with good advice.

Hence, this book is descriptive and analytical rather than prescriptive. It draws upon relevant research and scholarly literature to describe and explain objectively the process of group communication. It also deals with many of the more important group communication methodologies. Although skill development is not the major thrust of this book, it is hoped that the insights into small-group communication processes provided by this book, when supported by group communication activities in the classroom, will enable the student to improve his skills as a discussant.

acknowledgments

This textbook was conceived at a luncheon meeting with James H. Clark and Edward H. Stanford. Chancellor Maurice B. Mitchell and his administration's strong support of the speech communication program at the University of Denver made the effort possible. Edward A. Lindell, a most perceptive Dean, helped facilitate the project with his enthusiasm, trust and friendship. Franklyn S. Haiman and Dean C. Barnlund influenced the entire approach through their teaching and writing. Criticism of the manuscript and encouragement were provided by Larry L. Barker, Robert J. Kibler, and Mark L. Knapp.

Lacey Walker, Frieda Litvin, Carolyn Barrocas, Gail Hamilton, Marcia Sutton and Suzanne Kurtz played indispensable roles in the preparation of the materials, Edith Glickstein and Debra J. Kelley went out of their way to help with the typing of the final manuscript. The overall effort was enhanced by the warm and productive departmental atmosphere maintained by our speech communication students and colleagues.

Judy, Jonathan, Benjamin, Elissa, and Adam as well as Eva and Irvin provided the time and inspiration.

A.A.G.

GROUP COMMUNICATION

understanding
group
communication

the nature
of
group
communication

1

OBJECTIVES

After studying this chapter, you should be able to:

Describe the domain of group communication.

Differentiate between group communication and group dynamics, discussion, interpersonal communication, organizational communication, and laboratory training.

Define "discipline" and differentiate it from "field of study."

Identify the attributes and characteristics of group communication as a discipline.

With just a knife and a blanket, Sam said, he had been dumped in the middle of the Rocky Mountain wilderness. His objective was simply to survive. He had to live in the wilderness even though he might be hungry, bruised, afraid, and tired. This was the final examination for a two-week course in survival training that Sam had taken. He had been taught to locate and identify edible plants, to make pine tea, to dig wild turnips, to find sources of drinkable water, to stay warm, to conserve his energy, to maintain his bearings, and many other things. We listened as Sam described his unusual and somewhat harrowing experiences. The environment in which Sam had to survive was a strangely mixed one, beautiful yet hostile, a source of great personal satisfaction and a feeling of futility, alternately building and destroying self-confidence—an environment in which events occurred that were both expected and unpredictable, both routine and inexplicable.

The training he had received must have been helpful, for Sam survived. And if he ever again finds himself in the middle of the Rocky Mountain wilderness, the survival training will prove its worth. Yet we wonder how much help Sam has received for surviving in his other environments, the environments in which he finds himself every day.

Sams works hard and comes home tired. And it seems to Sam that he spends far too much of his time controlling the rotten crabgrass and weeds that mar the beauty of his otherwise perfect suburban yard. Sam thinks that mowing the lawn, trimming the edges, feeding the bushes, and clipping the hedges are poor substitutes for watching the football games. In fact Sam yearns to rip out everything and put a solid sheet of green asphalt around his house. But everytime he works up the nerve to do it, his neighbors tell him for the hundredth time how nicely kept his yard is. So Sam keeps digging and cursing.

Sam worked for almost a year on the plans for a new air filtration system in his foundry. Aside from the pleasure he would derive from making conditions safer and more pleasant for his fellow workers, Sam would get a pretty healthy chunk of money if his plans were used. And there was this boat, this beautiful boat, that most people would have to spend their whole lives working for. With the money Sam could buy it. So when the big day arrived for Sam to present his plans to the management committee, he naturally took some extra precautions. He explained his plans, in great detail, to each person on the committee and obtained informal assurances from each one, one at a time, that they would support his plans at the meeting. Thus, the afternoon after the committee met, Sam's wife was amazed to discover that his plans were not approved. She asked why. Sam was dazed, incoherent. Something happened during the meeting, but he didn't know what. The committee acted very strangely, but he couldn't explain it. After the meeting, the members of the committee were very friendly and extremely complimentary; each was apparently convinced that Sam had been screwed by "those other rotten bastards."

Sam is a member of a community businessmen's club. He considers most of the projects that the club undertakes to be worthwhile, and he enjoys the time he spends with the guys. But the meetings are unbearable. Much time seems to be wasted on irrelevant concerns. The officers seem inept. Half of the decisions made at one meeting are reversed at the next meeting. Frustration and chaos are the predominant moods. And at the last meeting, when Sam intervened in an attempt to help the group organize itself more productively, turmoil resulted and Sam got blamed for making matters worse. So Sam is going to quit. He has spent every night this week composing a bitter and impassioned letter to the club expressing his displeasure. The letter has been extremely difficult to write because Sam can't figure out exactly what's wrong or what's to be done about it.

All of us are like Sam. We all live in environments in which a form of survival is at stake. When we attend the meeting of a social club or a committee, it is not physical survival, but our personal psychological well-being which is threatened. The small group generates a great deal of frustration, disorientation, and dissatisfaction. And, as is the case with most social contexts, the small group is also a potential source of great personal reward, concrete accomplishments, and social stability. But any environment, if not understood, can be confusing, immobilizing, and threatening—a wilderness.

Like Sam, we have all experienced the small-group environment in many forms. And yet, if experience alone were sufficient for the development of understanding and social skills, then surely the experience you have already accumulated with small groups would be sufficient to give you a detailed understanding of group processes and the ability to effectively participate in small groups. Experience, though essential to learning, is rarely sufficient by itself. Usually, learning is optimized if experience is accompanied by a conceptual framework, a way of looking at things with labels that can be applied to help you recognize and order them. The conceptual base may seem pedestrian at first, as it always does when someone says, "The first thing you need to know is. . . ." Indeed, the beginning points of the conceptual base seemed pedestrian to us as we wrote this book. We kept wanting to rush ahead to later chapters where we would have an opportunity to deal with more complicated and intriguing group phenomena. Instead, we have decided to build slowly and deliberately toward an understanding of small-group processes because, in our judgment, there is no other social environment in greater need of understanding, or potentially as rewarding, or more difficult to cope with. Let us begin with some preliminary distinctions between group communication, the object of this volume, and other areas of study with which it is frequently confused.

Group communication is an area of study, research, and application that focuses not on group process in general, but on the communication behavior of individuals in small face-to-face discussion groups. We can ask a variety of questions about group communication, and the answers will help us better understand the boundaries and attributes of group communication.

Group Communication
versus Group Dynamics

How does group communication as an area of study and research differ from group dynamics? There is an obvious overlap. But whereas group dynamics is the study of many aspects of group behavior, group communication focuses on the communication process in small groups. Although the specialist in group communication examines many of the same variables that the group dynamicist is interested in, he approaches those variables in a different way. He examines them to determine how they influence or are influenced by the discussion or communication behavior of group members. This primary concern with the communication process in small groups also differentiates group communication from other areas of small-group study such as the sociology of small groups, group therapy, and the like.

Group Communication versus Discussion

How does group communication differ from discussion? Discussion has been an important area of study ever since McBurney and Hance published the first edition of *Discussion in Human Affairs* in 1939.[1] Group communication is a vital part of the discussion tradition and represents the inevitable next step in the development or evolution of group discussion as an area of study, research, and application in speech communication. Both group communication and group discussion focus on the discussion behavior of group members. Group communication, however, views the small-group discussion process from a more "scientific" point of view—more as an area of inquiry and somewhat less as an area of skill development and group improvement.

Group communication is more interested in the description and analysis of the discussion process than it is in prescriptions for enhancing a discussion group's effectiveness. This does not in any way mean that group communication is not concerned with ways in which the communication skills of group members can be improved. It merely means that the goals of skill development and group effectiveness are sought either directly or indirectly by examining the discussion process in a scientific

[1] James H. McBurney and Kenneth G. Hance, *Discussion in Human Affairs* (New York: Harper & Brothers, 1939).

or scholarly fashion rather than by formulating principles of good discussion or setting forth rules that the discussant who wants to improve
his performance should follow.

Group communication is the study of the way things are when
individuals interact with one another in small groups, not a description
of the way they ought to be plus a body of advice about how to make
them that way. However, it is quite conceivable from a group communication perspective that in the long run, an emphasis on description and
analysis may do more to improve group discussion processes than the
finest set of prescriptions ever could.

Group Communication
versus Interpersonal Communication

How does group communication differ from interpersonal communication? It is not necessary to draw a fine line between interpersonal communication and group communication. Both areas overlap and there
are many face-to-face situations that could be described either way
depending on the focus and purpose of the observer. In what ways are
the two areas similar? Both interpersonal and group communication
involve two or more individuals who are in physical proximity and who
generate and respond to each other's nonverbal and verbal cues and
messages.[2] But interpersonal communication generally refers to highly
spontaneous and relatively unstructured encounters of two, three, or
perhaps four individuals, whereas group communication refers to somewhat more structured situations in which the participants are more likely
to identify themselves as a group and where there is a greater awareness
of common goals. Group communication tends to be more deliberate
than interpersonal communication, and the participants are generally
more aware of their roles and responsibilities. Although group communication can and does occur in groups of two, three, or four, it also
occurs in larger face-to-face groups, and the groups are likely to be more
permanent than groups involved in interpersonal communication.

The major criteria, then, for differentiating between interpersonal
and group communication are amount of spontaneity, amount of structure, awareness of goals, group size, relative permanence of the group,
and sense of identity. It is possible, of course, to refer to interpersonal
events in a group communication setting, or vice versa, depending upon
the particular focus or concern of the observer.

[2]Dean C. Barnlund, *Interpersonal Communication* (Boston: Houghton Mifflin,
1968). pp. 8–10.

Group Communication
versus Organizational Communication

How does group communication differ from organizational communication? Many years ago, George Simmel wrote:

> smaller groups have qualities, including types of interaction among their members, which inevitably disappear when the groups grow larger.[3]

It would be difficult to challenge Simmel's assertion. Obviously, large organizations differ from small face-to-face groups in many ways. Obviously, too, there are similarities. There is no reason to believe, however, that a single theoretical system could not explain events on both the group and organizational levels. According to Cartright and Zander:

> both diads and triads can be dealt with effectively in terms of theories developed from investigations of larger groups. Moreover . . . conceptions of group dynamics derived from research on rather small groups can be successfully applied to groups having members numbered in the millions. Until better empirical evidence becomes available to establish a fundamental discontinuity along the dimension of size . . . it should not be assumed . . . that a single theoretical system cannot encompass face-to-face groups and organizations.[4]

But whether or not a single theoretical system will explain events on both a small-group and an organizational level, there are some major differences between group communication and organizational communication. Group communication is direct and face-to-face. Organizational communication need not be direct and often isn't. Group communication is less likely to be purged of emotion and more likely to involve interpersonal influence as opposed to the satisfaction of rational organizational goals.[5,6] Furthermore, communication in the small group is generally more spontaneous, less structured, and less goal-oriented than organizational communication. Organizational communication, on the

[3]George Simmel, "The Significance of Numbers for Social Life," in *In Small Groups*, rev. ed., ed. A. Paul Hare, Edgar F. Borgatta, and Robert F. Bales (New York: Knopf, 1965), p. 10.

[4]Dorwin Cartright and Alvin Zander, eds., *Group Dynamics*, 2d ed. (New York: Harper & Row, 1960), pp. 37–38.

[5]Robert T. Golembiewski, *Behavior and Organization* (Chicago: Rand McNally, 1962).

[6]Robert T. Golembiewski, *The Small Group* (Chicago: University of Chicago Press, 1962).

other hand, is more likely to occur in a permanent setting and to reflect a greater sense of identity than small-group communication.

Group Communication
versus Laboratory Training

What is the relationship between group communication and laboratory training? Laboratory training refers to a variety of small-group approaches to self-awareness, understanding others, and to the improvement of group operations that began with the establishment of the National Training Laboratories (NTL) in the late 1940s. These approaches are also referred to as T-group training, sensitivity training, encounter, etc. Students of group communication are interested in laboratory training from two perspectives. They are interested in how individuals communicate with one another in laboratory settings and in why they interact that way. They are also interested in the value and effectiveness of laboratory training as a methodology for improving the communication skills or behavior of small-group members. Laboratory approaches to group communication are dealt with more extensively in Chapter 8 of this text.

The Discipline of Group Communication

Elwood Murray, one of the pioneers in speech communication, has pointed out that a discipline is more than just a domain or field study. To be a discipline, an area of scholarship should have five basic ingredients. A discipline requires (1) a domain or territory, (2) a theory or theories, (3) a research methodology, (4) a criticism, and (5) an application.[7] On the basis of these criteria, group communication is well on its way to becoming a discipline, or at least a subdiscipline within speech communication. The following section considers how each of these criteria applies to group communication.

THE DOMAIN

Much of this chapter has been devoted to a description of the domain and an identification of the boundaries of group communication. We have clarified the differences and the relationships between group com-

[7]Elwood Murray, unpublished lecture (1972).

munication and group dynamics, discussion, interpersonal communication, organizational communication, and laboratory training. We have also identified the types of groups that group communication is interested in. The general concern of group communication is with the small group. But unlike group dynamics, sociology, psychology, social psychology, and other areas that examine small-group processes, group communication is the only discipline that focuses primarily on communication phenomena in small groups. The group communication specialist is interested in how individuals in face-to-face group situations communicate. He seeks to better understand the process of group communication and to better predict the outcomes of group communication. But the domain of group communication is more than a normative one. In addition to understanding and prediction, the group communication specialist seeks control. That is, he seeks ways to improve the group communication process. This interest in training and improvement is treated more fully later in this chapter in the discussion of application.

THEORY

Group communication specialists are interested in scientific theory building. They recognize fully the importance of theory in the development of a discipline. Group communication can grow and develop in a systematic and meaningful way only if the efforts of group communication researchers, teachers, and practitioners can be given direction, clarity of purpose, and coherency through theory. Theory will not only provide researchers with hypotheses to test; it will also enable them to make sense out of the data they collect and allow them to synthesize the findings of other researchers. At the present time, the authors know of no explicit and comprehensive theories of group communication that have been published by speech communication scholars. Chapter 4 of this text identifies some of the implicit theoretical assumptions that have guided group communication scholars.

RESEARCH METHODOLOGY

There are many ways of knowing. Intuitive, mystical, and authoritarian methods are at times, no doubt, very worthwhile strategies for achieving certainty and eliminating doubt. But, over the years, the commitment of group communication scholars has been to scientific methods—to pragmatism, empiricism, and rationalism. There may be no ultimate way of justifying this commitment other than by peer-group agreement or faith, but we are convinced that there is no better alternative than the scientific method when answers are sought to the factual questions the group communication specialist asks about communication processes in small groups. Historical and critical methods are also important to us when we ask questions about our past or make critical judgments about group training procedures or techniques for facilitating a group's communication.

The authors of this text have used experimental methods to study group communication and will continue to do so. But descriptive methods that involve the analysis of messages and the careful observation of existing groups may be more valuable at this stage in the development of the discipline than carefully controlled studies where some variables are manipulated while others are held constant.

CRITICISM

When scientists deny the value of critical approaches to knowledge, they object primarily to speculation or armchair philosophizing about factual questions that can best be answered by using empirical methods. We can speculate all we want, for example, about the effects an authoritarian leader has on the communication of group members, but until we actually observe and measure these effects, we will never really know if our speculations are accurate. There are certain questions, however, that cannot be answered scientifically. These are questions related to the goodness and badness or the rightness and wrongness of something. Scientific data may help us make a judgment, but scientific methods and the data they generate do not provide that judgment. To judge the worth of something, we must use critical methods. Fortunately, this is an area where members of the speech communication discipline have excelled. Critical research and the development of critical standards for guiding communication events and judging communication behaviors have long been a major part of the speech communication tradition.

Criticism is relevant to the development of a discipline because it enables the members of that discipline to examine and improve their assumptions, theories, research methods, and applications. The increasing emphasis in group communication on descriptive rather than experimental methods and the expanding interest in message variables grow out of a critical appraisal of the theoretical and methodological interests of group communication scholars. On the applied level, critical standards that were developed over the years by discussion teachers and scholars provide a basis for judging and improving the communication behavior of discussants and discussion groups.

APPLICATION

Group communication is one of the few disciplines that had an application and a criticism before it had a clearly defined domain, theory, or research methodology. Courses in discussion were developed and taught on college campuses during the past forty years because, among other reasons, individuals and groups felt a need to improve their group communication skills. These skills include proficiency in reflective thinking, reasoning, listening, speaking, role playing, case analysis, climate making, leadership, and the like. The applications of group communication have gone far beyond the college classroom to include conferences and workshops for industrial organizations, professional groups, and the community. These workshops or conferences deal with leadership, conflict resolution, motivation, interpersonal relations, self-concept, self-awareness, and a variety of other matters related to personal growth and group development.

If we use the reasonable standards suggested by Elwood Murray as our criteria, then group communication can be described as a discipline. It has a domain, it is making progress in the development of theory, and it has a research methodology, a criticism, and an application. The various chapters in this book elaborate on developments in all of these areas.

SUMMARY

1. Group communication focuses primarily on communication phenomena in small groups—on how to better understand the process of group communication and predict outcomes and on how to improve the group communication process.

2. Whereas group dynamics is the study of many aspects of group behavior, group communication focuses on the communication process per se in small groups.

3. Whereas group discussion offers various prescriptions for the improvement of group communication skills, group communication places the emphasis on description and analysis. Both are concerned with group effectiveness and skill development in the long run.

4. Whereas interpersonal communication generally refers to highly spontaneous, unstructured encounters between two to four people, group communication refers to more structured situations where participants identify themselves as a group and are more aware of common goals.

5. As opposed to organizational communication, group communication is more likely to involve interpersonal and emotional influence, is more likely to occur directly through face-to-face encounter, and is more spontaneous, less structured, and less goal-oriented.

6. Laboratory training refers to a variety of small-group approaches to increasing self-awareness, to understanding others, and to improving group operations.

7. According to Murray, five components are necessary for a field of study to be called a discipline: a domain or territory, a theory or theories, a research methodology, a criticism, and an application. According to these criteria group communication can be described as a discipline.

group communication research: the speech communication perspective

2

OBJECTIVES

After studying this chapter, you should be able to:

State two principal questions dealt with in the research conducted by speech communication researchers.

Identify some of the questions posed by speech communication researchers.

State some of the conclusions the research has generated.

Begin to see group communication phenomena as something other than random disorder that is incapable of being understood or systematically explained.

There is always at least a little wisdom in most old aphorisms. "He couldn't see the forest for the trees," or "we don't know who discovered water, but we can be sure that it wasn't a fish," or "if you want to hide something choose the most obvious place," are all shorthand ways of saying that the more pervasive and always-present phenomena are frequently the last to be discovered and explained. Such is surely the case with the phenomenon called "communication." It would be difficult to identify another process more central to all forms of human activity. Few other processes are more instrumental in determining the kinds of individuals we become, the identities we forge for ourselves, the values we adhere to, the life-long goals for which we work, the kinds of insti-

tutions and societies we construct, and the eventual maintenance or
destruction of these institutions and societies. That communication is
one of the most central and important processes is being increasingly
recognized. But the pervasiveness of the process has made such recognition of very recent origin. The systematic investigation of human
communication, in serious theoretical and scientific activities coordinated
within and between academic units, is a comparatively recent development. Man is now becoming intrigued by the element in which he has
been immersed throughout his history as a social creature.

Systematic attempts to understand the communication behavior of
individuals in groups are also of comparatively recent origin. In the
early part of this century intense interest in group processes was generated by the "discovery" of a new educational method. The most
popular name for this new method was "group discussion." Individuals
with varying perspectives collected their particular academic armaments
in an effort to make of this method an innovative and progressive approach to the use of human resources. From Eubank's survey of periodical literature on group discussion, we can judge that three major
approaches to the subject area existed between 1900 and 1935.[1] First,
members of the education discipline, in great numbers and in a wide
range of professional journals, argued the merits of group discussion as
a teaching-learning device. Second, psychologists began to explore, in
relatively controlled laboratory experiments, some of the variables assumed to be related to small-group processes. Third, individuals in the
speech field argued about the specific uses to which group discussion
might be put—for example, students might use it to acquire the attitudes
and habits of scientific thinking, teachers could use it to elicit greater
involvement and interest from their students, and audiences could use
it to obtain information and more solid foundations upon which to
build attitudes related to a given topic.

In these early years, the attention of speech communication teachers
and researchers focused upon public forms of discussion. Students were
taught how to plan, prepare for, and participate in panel discussions
and symposia. Researchers investigated the effects of public discussions
on the attitudes and information acquisition of audiences, as well as
the effects of public discussions on the attitudes of participants and the
comparative effectiveness of various public discussion formats. The
heavy emphasis on public discussion, however, has disappeared and has
been replaced by a heavy emphasis on small groups meeting privately to
solve problems and make decisions. Bormann has stated, "historically,

---

[1]Henry Lee Eubank, "Bibliography of Periodical Literature on Debating and
Discussion," *Quarterly Journal of Speech* 24 (1938): 634–41.

the trend has been from a heavy loading of public discussion toward more emphasis on the small group meeting as a mechanism for collecting and processing information and for making decisions."[2] Taylor's survey of group discussion courses in selected American colleges and universities supports Bormann's conclusion.[3] Our own recent summary of research reported in speech communication journals suggests that contemporary speech communication research on small groups is directed primarily toward answering two questions: (1) What basic processes describe group communication; that is, what happens when people interact in small groups? (2) What factors determine or allow us to account for the outcomes of group communication; that is, what group communication variables are associated with more successful, more effective, or more rewarding group communication activities?[4] To illustrate the speech communication perspective, let us examine the research related to these two questions.

Group Communication Processes

There is an almost unlimited number of answers to the question, What happens when individuals interact in small groups? You may be able to provide many answers yourself. After all, unless you are a dedicated recluse, you have probably participated in many small groups whose interests have ranged from a task orientation to a social orientation. If your accumulated experiences have not resulted in some answers to the question of what happens when individuals interact in small groups, there are probably some reasonable explanations. One explanation is that so much happens all at once that it is difficult to make sense out of rapidly occurring, intertwining, and overlapping events that confront an individual when he participates in group communication activities. Another explanation is that you might not have been equipped with labels to give to the phenomena that were occurring; or you might not have been equipped with conceptual distinctions which would allow you to see the total process in terms of some of its components. Consequently, our strategy at this point should be twofold. (1) We should attempt to isolate, from among the many processes occurring simultaneously in group communication, some of the simpler and more com-

2Ernest G. Bormann, "Pedagogic Space: A Strategy for Teaching Discussion," *The Speech Teacher* 19 (1970): 274.

3James S. Taylor, "A Study of Group Discussion in Selected American Colleges and Universities," *Southern Speech Journal* 33 (1967): 113–18.

4Carl E. Larson, "Speech Communication Research on Small Groups," *The Speech Teacher* 20 (1971): 89–107.

prehensible processes. (2) We should employ some conceptual tags or labels which will allow us to organize our observations. The research reported in the remainder of this section represents the attempts of particular investigators, each with his own perspective, to isolate some basic process variables and to label them.

Berg observed 124 discussions by thirty-nine separate religious, political, professional, and education groups.[5] Berg analyzed the content of these discussions by coding the themes discussed by the groups into the following categories:

1. Substantive themes were those related topically to the task.
2. Procedural themes were those concerning how the discussions should progress, be organized, or be changed or corrected.
3. Irrelevant themes were those which did not relate substantially or procedurally to the task.
4. Disruptions were occurrences which interrupted the themes being discussed, for example, when two or more members talked at the same time.

Task themes (substantive and procedural) comprised 84.2 percent of the total number of themes introduced, and occupied 91.7 percent of the total group time. Nontask themes (irrelevant and disruptive) comprised 15.8 percent of the number of themes introduced and occupied 8.3 percent of the total group time. As might be expected, classroom groups were characterized by a greater number of procedural themes than were the other types of groups. Although it might appear that a small group is accomplishing its purposes by simply discussing the content of a given problem confronting the group, we will contend that one of the most important determinants of the adequacy of small-group discussion is the manner in which procedural issues are raised and resolved by group members.

Scheidel and Crowell analyzed the interaction generated by five groups, each of which met for six hours to evaluate a metropolitan newsletter.[6] Observers identified and coded "thought-units," the smallest ideational contributions made by the participants. The researchers discovered that a relatively small amount of time was devoted to the initiation, extension, modification, and synthesis of ideas (only 22 percent of the thought-units fell in these categories). One-fourth of all participant comments were statements accepting ideas already before

[5]David M. Berg, "A Descriptive Analysis of the Distribution and Duration of Themes Discussed by Task-Oriented Small Groups," *Speech Monographs* 34 (1967): 172–75.

[6]Thomas M. Scheidel and Laura Crowell, "Idea Development in Small Discussion Groups," *Quarterly Journal of Speech* 50 (1964): 140–45.

the group. Another one-fourth of the thought-units were devoted to clarifying and substantiating ideas already before the group. The researchers described group thought as exhibiting a "reach-test" motion. That is, "one participant reaches forth with an inference which seems to be elaborated at length with movements of clarification, substantiation, and verbalized acceptance."

In order to better understand this "reach-test" motion, we should examine another of Scheidel and Crowell's findings. After performing a contiguity analysis of the thought-units (a contiguity analysis is one which attempts to determine the probabilities with which a given event will tend to follow a given other event), researchers concluded that assertions in these discussions were about 80 percent as unpredictable as they could be. In other words, knowledge of specific antecedent events does not seem to provide us with a very good basis for predicting what events will occur subsequently. Based upon your own experience, you might agree that group communication often appears disconnected and fragmented, with group members groping, in an almost trial-and-error manner, to present thoughts that will be acceptable to other group members.

In another investigation Scheidel and Crowell focused specifically on feedback events occurring in small discussion groups.[7] Defining a feedback event as "that event in which any participant (X) initiates a comment which is followed by a comment from any other participant (Y) which in turn is followed immediately by a further comment from the first participant (X)," these researchers discovered that approximately one-third of the total interaction consisted of feedback activity. When feedback did occur, the process was characterized by comments of agreement or comments directed toward minor aspects of the discussion content. The feedback process did not seem to prompt group members to change directions, modify thinking, or substantiate ideas.

Some additional information on sequences of member communicative acts is available from the research of Stech.[8] Stech analyzed the utterances of three-member groups confronted with the task of ranking fourteen types of music in the order in which the average American factory worker would prefer the types of music. The category system employed to code types of member utterances was a relatively simple one, developed specifically for the ranking task. Thus, the groups were small, the category system relatively simple, and the task one from which stereotypical patterns of interaction might be assumed to emerge. Even

[7]Thomas M. Scheidel and Laura Crowell, "Feedback in Small Group Communication," *Quarterly Journal of Speech* 52 (1966): 273–78.

[8]Ernest L. Stech, "An Analysis of Interaction Structure in the Discussion of a Ranking Task," *Speech Monographs* 37 (1970): 249–56.

so, Stech's analysis disclosed very little predictability with respect to which kinds of member utterances would follow which other kinds of member utterances. Stech's results may be summarized as indicating that approximately one-third of the member utterances could be predicted from a knowledge of what preceded the utterances.

Some clarification of the contiguity research is necessary at this point. First, the orientation of contiguity researchers is to describe group communication processes by categorizing member statements or utterances into different "classes" or "types." Sequential relationships among different classes of verbal utterances are then analyzed. Second, the somewhat random and nonpredictable picture of group communication processes which emerges from contiguity research would not necessarily hold among research which has adopted a different orientation or a different level of analysis. For example, Bostrom has found considerable structure in the sending and receiving behavior of group members.[9] Who talks to whom and with what frequency are matters which appear to be quite systematic. Additionally, that the basic question of who sends and receives messages and with what frequency is an important one is demonstrated by Bostrom's findings that: (1) Group members who send more messages are more likely to be identified by other members as "leaders," even though the group may have initially been "leaderless." (2) Members who send more messages are more likely to be identified by other group members as "good discussants." (3) Members who send more messages are more likely to be satisfied with the group process. From one legitimate point of view, then, a group's structure may be seen as emerging from "who talks to whom and with what frequency." Our third comment on contiguity research is that whereas the classes or categories of utterances which group members exhibit may not be systematically related to each other, group communication processes may nevertheless be quite systematic and predictable if one changes his level of analysis to focus on the phases through which groups move in their discussion of a problem. Among the more relevant research on phases in group deliberations is that of Fisher.[10]

Fisher's investigation, which included but was not restricted to contiguity analysis, was an attempt to discover whether decision-making groups could be characterized by a basic interaction process. Fisher studied groups of differing sizes, types, and compositions. The category system through which verbal behavior of group members was coded was

[9]Robert N. Bostrom, "Patterns of Communicative Interaction in Small Groups," *Speech Monographs* 37 (1970): 257–63.

[10]B. Aubrey Fisher, " 'Decision Emergence.' Phases in Group Decision-Making," *Speech Monographs* 37 (1970): 53–66; idem, "The Process of Decision Modification in Small Discussion Groups," *Journal of Communication* 20 (1970): 51–64.

related primarily to the concept of a "decision proposal." The basic process operating in decision-making groups is considered to be a process wherein alternative decision proposals are advanced and responded to by group members. The core of Fisher's category system deals with the extent to which decision proposals are interpreted, substantiated, clarified, modified, summarized, or agreed with, or result in favorable, unfavorable, or ambiguous responses. Fisher's investigation led him to identify a relative consistent pattern of four phases through which group deliberations move.

PHASE ONE: ORIENTATION

In the initial phase of a group's deliberations members are uncertain about how acceptable their ideas will be to other group members. Assertions are made tentatively and opinions are expressed cautiously. Much of the verbal behavior is directed toward clarifying decision proposals and expressing agreement with statements made by other group members. Ambiguous comments and ambiguous interpretations tend to elicit more agreement in this first phase than in subsequent phases. Even unfavorable comments tend to be agreed with more in the first phase than in subsequent phases. This overriding tendency to agree with nearly everything seems to represent a tentative search for ideas and directions as well as an attempt to avoid disrupting an already tenuously established group climate. Ideas are expressed without much substantiation. Ambiguous comments are reinforced. Group members do not reinforce predominantly any single decision proposal. Getting acquainted, clarifying, and tentatively expressing attitudes seem to characterize the first phase.

PHASE TWO: CONFLICT

The second phase is characterized by dispute. Unfavorable opinions, substantiations, and interpretations increase during this period. Opinions are much more definite. Ambiguous comments decrease. The relevant decision proposals seem to have been identified, and group members adopt argumentative stances, both favorable and unfavorable, toward these proposals. Unfavorable responses to decision proposals are countered by favorable comments. The comments are expressed more tenaciously. Decision proposals are not interpreted as extensively as they were in phase one; instead, they are substantiated with information and data directed toward persuading disagreeing group members. Coalitions form. Positions become polarized. The phase is characterized by conflict.

PHASE THREE: EMERGENCE

Conflict, and the accompanying unfavorable comments, decline during phase three. Comments and decision proposals are interpreted more frequently, and such interpretation is reinforced by immediately subsequent interpretations. Members do not defend themselves as tenaciously against unfavorable comments. Considerable ambiguity returns. Whereas ambiguity was related to the expression of tentative attitudes in phase one, ambiguity in phase three is a form of "modified dissent." Member attitudes are changing from disapproval to approval of some decision proposals. The heightened ambiguity in phase three seems to be a function of the attitude change which is occurring in this phase. Initially unfavorable attitudes are expressed somewhat ambiguously now. The emergence of certain decision proposals as preferred proposals can be seen in this phase.

PHASE FOUR: REINFORCEMENT

Preferred decision proposals become increasingly visible during phase four. Argument is replaced by reinforcement. This phase contains more favorable interpretation of decision proposals than does the preceding phase. More favorable substantiation occurs. The emphasis on reinforcement can be seen in an increased number of sequences of comments favoring a decision proposal. Dissent disappears. Ambiguous comments decline. Ambiguous comments are typically not reinforced in this phase. Members are striving for agreement and tend to reinforce one another with respect to agreement on specific decision proposals. The final phase is characterized by a spirit of unity, and there is an apparent avoidance or relatively quick disposal of comments and proposals which threaten to take the group back through conflict and argumentative processes.

There are many phase models of group processes. Our own experience with problem-solving and decision-making groups supports Fisher's descriptions. Additionally, Fisher's model seems more clearly descriptive of the speech communication behavior of group members than are other models.

Our attempt so far has been to paint a realistic picture of group communication processes. Our treatment of the topic is by no means complete, and there is more to follow. Now, however, several points need reinforcing. First, group communication processes are, to a certain extent, confusing, perhaps mildly frustrating, and somewhat unpredictable. To deny this point is to deny a conclusion compelled upon us by our own experience. On the other hand, we believe, and have attempted to point out, that group communication processes are not totally random, do not defy systematic explanation, and can be understood. In pursuing this understanding, our next step is to review some selected speech communication research which has attempted to identify factors related to individual communication behavior in small groups.

Factors Related to
Member Communicative Behavior

One strategy frequently employed in group communication research is the use of peer ratings, usually consisting of member judgments of others' effectiveness as discussion participants. These judgments are used as the basis for distinguishing between high- and low-rated participants. We are not quite sure what criteria group members use when they rate each other's effectiveness as discussion participants, but whatever it is in the behavior of discussion participants which leads to higher ratings, such higher-rated participants differ from lower-rated participants in a number of ways. For example, higher-rated participants seem to have more confidence in their skill as communicators.[11] Higher-rated participants seem to be less satisfied with the process and with the product of group deliberations.[12] And higher-rated participants seem to have less need for forming or maintaining social affiliations but more need for recognition as influential members of the group.[13] That higher-rated participants are characterized by a greater need for recognition as influential members of the group is not surprising. But that higher-rated participants have less need for forming or maintaining social affiliations is, perhaps, an unexpected finding.

The relationship between sociability and group communication processes is an interesting one. This relationship is further elaborated in an investigation by Lerea and Goldberg.[14] Lerea and Goldberg investigated groups composed of students who had scored either in the upper quartile or the lower quartile on a scale purporting to measure

[11]Laura Crowell, Allen Katcher, and S. Frank Miyamoto, "Self-Concepts of Communication Skill and Performance in Small Group Discussions," *Speech Monographs* 22 (1955): 20–27.

[12]Laura Crowell and Thomas M. Scheidel, "A Study of Discussant Satisfaction in Group Problem Solving," *Speech Monographs* 30 (1963): 56–88.

[13]Thomas M. Scheidel, Laura Crowell, and John P. Shepherd, "Personality and Discussion Behavior: A Study of Possible Relationships," *Speech Monographs* 25 (1958): 261–67.

[14]Louis Lerea and Alvin Goldberg, "The Effects of Socialization Upon Group Behavior," *Speech Monographs* 28 (1961): 60–64.

tendencies to enter into or to withdraw from social contact with others. The students, in 5-member groups, engaged in fifty-minute discussions on "the role of the student in determining University Policy;" the groups consisted of various combinations of high-sociability and low-sociability members. Among other things, Lerea and Goldberg found that less inter-action occurred in all low-sociability or all high-sociability groups, and that as the number of high-sociability members increased, member satis-faction with the group performance and intermember social attractiveness decreased. In this and other related studies, researchers have provided evidence that highly "sociable" members of groups somehow seem to affect, comparatively negatively, member satisfaction with the group's performance or with the "sociable" members.

Occasionally, such nonobvious findings creep into the research on group communication. For example, one factor which has been demon-strated to affect group communication processes is the nature and source of evaluations confronting groups. Goldberg found that groups of partic-ipants who believe themselves to be evaluated either positively or negatively by their peers subsequently became more process-oriented (attended to and discussed the internal operations and characteristics of the group itself); in contrast, groups evaluated positively by external observers became less process-oriented, and groups evaluated negatively by external observers became more task-oriented (attended to and dis-cussed issues related to the content of the task confronting the group).[15]

Gouran has adopted a somewhat different strategy for investigating communication processes.[16] Groups composed of six college students discussed one of the following policy questions: the University of Iowa's policies on undergraduate women's hours, undergraduates' possession of automobiles, and grading. A total of five alternative conclusions with respect to each policy was available to group members. For each ques-tion, two groups were identified. One of the groups had reached con-sensus (a unanimous agreement on a single policy), while the other group showed no significant movement toward consensus. Thus, the basic strategy was to identify one "consensus" group and one "no con-sensus" group for each question, and then to analyze the discussion of these groups to determine if the groups differed with respect to specific communication variables.

Eight variables were chosen for investigation. These variables were defined as follows:

15Alvin Goldberg, "An Experimental Study of the Effects of Evaluation Upon Group Behavior," *Quarterly Journal of Speech* 46 (1960): 274–83.
16Dennis S. Gouran, "Variables Related to Consensus in Group Discussions of Questions of Policy," *Speech Monographs* 36 (1969): 387–91.

1. Clarity. A statement is said to be clear when an individual hearing or reading it feels confident that he understands what its maker means.
2. Opinionatedness. A statement is said to be opinionated when it expresses a feeling, belief, or judgment, the factual basis for which is not apparent in the statement itself.
3. Interest. A statement is said to reflect the interest of its maker if it contains some indication of concern or involvement on his part with the question being discussed.
4. Amount of information. A statement is said to be informative if it contains facts, statistics, and opinions of qualified sources which bear directly on some aspect of the question being discussed.
5. Provocativeness. A statement is said to be provocative if it reflects a desire or willingness on the part of its maker to have another person make an overt response to it; that is, it seems to invite or welcome responses.
6. Orientation. A statement is said to give orientation if it reflects an attempt on the part of its maker to facilitate achievement of a group goal by using facts, making helpful suggestions, or trying to resolve conflict.
7. Objectivity. A statement is said to be objective when it reflects freedom from conscious attempts on the part of its maker to persuade or otherwise influence another person or persons toward his point of view.
8. Length. Length is simply the number of words in a statement.[17]

Randomly selected statements from each of the discussions were transcribed from recordings of the discussions and judged according to the criteria listed above. For each topic of discussion, consensus and nonconsensus groups were compared using each of these eight variables.

Statements of consensus groups did not differ from statements of nonconsensus groups in either clarity (1) or length (8). Consensus groups did differ, however, from nonconsensus groups in terms of the extent to which orientation (6) and objectivity (7) were present. Consensus groups were characterized by higher levels of objectivity in the statements made by group members and by the tendency for their statements to provide more orientation, to be directed more to the achievement of the group goal, to make more helpful suggestions, or to be directed toward resolving conflict. Relationships between consensus and other variables were less clear and depended upon which particular topic the groups were discussing. That orientation and objectivity should be positively related to group consensus is not surprising. More unexpected, however, was the fact that clear-cut conclusions with respect to other variables did not emerge. Nevertheless, Gouran's investigation demonstrates that certain

17Ibid., p. 388.

process variables may help us to account for outcomes such as group consensus.

There are, of course, other investigations and descriptions of group communication processes. Some of these descriptions we wish to treat in greater detail, especially those which focus specifically on types of communication behavior engaged in by small-group members. Chapter 5, "Observing Group Communication," is our attempt to make much more explicit and understandable some of the important factors which make up and determine group communication processes.

Problem-Solving and Judgment Processes

An early focus of group communication research, and one which persists today, is the analysis of group communication as it relates to problem solving. The largest single cluster of early studies in group communication centered in this area. Dickens and Heffernan have suggested that the following conclusions were "well established" in the first phases of group communication research:

1. After discussion, extreme judgments tend to draw in toward a middle ground.
2. After discussion, judgments tend to improve in accuracy or correctness.
3. A great deal of influence upon an individual's judgment is exerted by knowledge of how the majority stands.
4. Right answers tend to be held more tenaciously than wrong ones, under same conditions of majority.
5. Group superiority is greater in dealing with problems permitting a greater range of responses.[18]

With these conclusions as points of departure, researchers focused their attention upon factors which might influence the effectiveness of problem-solving deliberations in small groups. One factor which attracted early attention was the "reflective thinking abilities" of participants.

REFLECTIVE THINKING ABILITY

Descriptions of reflective thinking processes suggested by John Dewey should be credited with providing the impetus for research on problem-solving processes in small groups.[19] Proceeding under the assumption

[18]Milton Dickens and Marguerite Heffernan, "Experimental Research in Group Discussion," *Quarterly Journal of Speech* 35 (1949): 23–29.
[19]John Dewey, *How We Think* (Boston: D. C. Heath, 1910).

that individuals confronted with a problem usually employ a pattern of thinking through that problem, and that this pattern proceeds through five phases,[20] Johnson devised a test which would provide researchers with some indication of how effectively an individual employs "reflective thinking" in his problem deliberations.[21]

Johnson's "How Do You Think" test attempts to measure aspects of the entire reflective thinking process. Form A confronts subjects with the problem of developing admission requirements for a privately endowed liberal arts college. Form B requires subjects to outline academic requirements for degrees from the same college. In reporting on the validity of this test Johnson states that the test has been subjected to various validity checks, producing data supportive of the following conclusions: (1) It has distinguished between groups of college students according to college years. (2) It has successfully discriminated among students according to amount of training in "logical thinking and scientific method." (3) It correlates highly with instructor judgments of student reasoning abilities. Several investigators, employing this test, have explored the relationships between the reflective thinking ability of participants and various outcomes of problem-solving group discussions.

Pyron and Sharp administered this test to students in a basic speech course who, in small groups, participated in two fifty-minute problem-solving discussions.[22] The students were ranked by instructors, student observers, and other group members according to "contributions made in achieving the group's goal." The high- and low-ranked discussion participants differed significantly on their reflective thinking test scores when instructor rankings were employed and when observer rankings were employed, and this relationship was "almost significant" when the rankings were made by other group members.

Relationships between reflective thinking ability and member rankings of participation effectiveness were found by Pyron in business and professional conferences.[23] Participants in business and professional conferences and discussions who were ranked in the lower third by fellow

[20]The five phases described by Dewey were: (1) a felt difficulty; (2) its location and definition; (3) suggestions of possible solutions; (4) development by reasoning of the bearings of the suggestions; (5) further observation and experiment leading to its acceptance or rejection, that is, the conclusion of belief or disbelief.

[21]Alma Johnson, "An Experimental Study in the Analysis and Measurement of Reflective Thinking," *Speech Monographs* 10 (1943): 83–96.

[22]H. Charles Pyron and Harry Sharp, Jr., "A Quantitative Study of Reflective Thinking and Performance in Problem-Solving Discussion," *Journal of Communication* 13 (1963): 46–57.

[23]H. Charles Pyron, "An Experimental Study of the Role of Reflective Thinking in Business and Professional Conferences and Discussions," *Speech Monographs* 31 (1964): 155–61.

participants scored significantly lower on the reflective thinking test than did those ranked in the middle or upper third.

Focusing their attention on the quality of the group's decision rather than on rankings of discussion participants, Sharp and Millikin attempted to determine whether groups composed of only high scorers, only medium scorers, or only low scorers on the reflective thinking test would differ in terms of the quality of the group's decision.[24] General educational policy problems were discussed by groups of high, medium, and low scorers. Each group discussed a different problem for three fifty-minute sessions with their objective defined as the preparation of a three- to four-page typed report of their suggestions on the problem. These reports were submitted to eighteen expert judges selected for their substantive competence in the problem areas, six judges reviewing reports on one of the three problems. The reports were ranked in terms of the quality of the group's analysis and recommendations. The results of this study disclosed that the quality of the group's decision was related to the reflective thinking ability of group members.

Two points seem reasonably well supported: (1) group members possessing higher levels of reflective thinking ability may be judged to be more effective group communication participants, and (2) groups composed of members all of whom score high on reflective thinking tests may produce higher-quality decisions. Consequently, it is tempting to assume that if a group collectively follows a reflective thinking pattern the quality of its problem-solving deliberations may improve. This is not necessarily the case. On an individual basis, reflective thinking ability may be positively related to certain products of problem-solving discussion. When the reflective thinking steps are explicitly stated so that the group as a whole follows a reflective thinking outline in their problem-solving deliberations, the research has produced results much more equivocal.

Bayless found no evidence that a reflective thinking pattern affected the accuracy of the final group solution, as determined by expert judgments.[25] Larson found only a slight difference between the accuracy of solution for groups employing a reflective thinking pattern as compared with groups employing no systematic problem-solving pattern.[26] Larson found, however, that two more recently developed problem-solving patterns each produced more accurate solutions than did a reflective thinking pattern. The traditional focus on reflective thinking, as well

---

[24]Harry Sharp, Jr. and Joyce Millikin, "Reflective Thinking Ability and the Product of Problem-Solving Discussion," *Speech Monographs* 31 (1964): 124–27.

[25]Ovid L. Bayless, "An Alternate Pattern for Problem-Solving Discussion," *Journal of Communication* 17 (1967): 188–97.

[26]Carl E. Larson, "Forms of Analysis and Small Group Problem-Solving," *Speech Monographs* 36 (1969): 452–55.

as alternative analysis patterns, are considered in much greater detail in Chapter 7, "Group Communication for Problem Solving."

Much of the communication research on small groups deals with factors which may be related to outcomes of problem-solving discussion. For the moment, however, we wish to consider some rather specific factors which have been studied in relative isolation from the greater number of variables purported to be related to group communication outcomes.

One of the early studies focused on relationships between sex differences and problem-solving outcomes.[27] Groups consisting of matched pairs of male and female subjects ranked problem solutions, and the rankings were compared for "accuracy" with ranks arrived at by eleven experts. Both males and females changed significantly in the accuracy of their rankings from before to after discussion. The increase in accuracy for females was considerably greater than for males. When rankings were obtained one month after the deliberations, both males and females had still maintained a significant increase in accuracy, but the females had lost some of their advantage over the males.

Most of the research on factors related to problem-solving discussion focuses on characteristics of the process rather than on characteristics of the participants. Keltner suggests that the effectiveness of problem-solving deliberations is related to a number of factors associated with the identification by group members of goals and obstacles within the problem situation.[28] To the extent that members explore the nature of the problem situation, attempt to identify specific goals for the group, and identify their status in relationship to these obstacles and goals, the group's deliberations are more effective.

We have already referred to several studies which explored the relationships between problem-solving patterns and discussion outcomes. In one investigation, the researchers were interested in whether, after a group conducts an initial analysis of a problem, the group will be more effective if it generates a possible solution before—as opposed to after—it establishes criteria by which to judge solutions.[29] Twenty-seven groups of five members each discussed three problems under the direction of a

27William M. Timmons, "Sex Differences in Discussion," *Speech Monographs* 8 (1941): 68–75.

28John W. Keltner, "Goals, Obstacles, and Problem Formulation in Group Discussion," *Quarterly Journal of Speech* 33 (1947): 468–73.

29John K. Brilhart and Lurene M. Jochem, "Effects of Different Patterns on Outcomes of Problem-Solving Discussion," *Journal of Applied Psychology* 48 (1964): 175–79.

leader trained in guiding the group through a specified problem-solving pattern. All groups discussed all three problems under three specified problem-solving patterns: (1) ideation-criteria, wherein possible solutions are generated before criteria are established for evaluating the solution; (2) criteria-ideation; and (3) solution, wherein the suggestion of solutions and their evaluation occur more or less concurrently. Outcome measures included: participant responses to questions concerning their satisfaction with the group's decisions, the designated leader, and the procedures followed; the number of ideas rated good by each of two experts; and number of solutions suggested. The results of this study include the following: (1) The ideation-criteria and criteria-ideation patterns both yielded approximately 50 percent more ideas than did the pattern in which suggestion of solutions and their evaluation were combined. (2) The ideation-criteria pattern yielded significantly more good ideas than did the combined solution and evaluation pattern. (3) Satisfaction with solutions, leaders, and patterns did not differ significantly in any of the cross-comparisons; however, significantly more subjects expressed preference for the ideation-criteria or the simple solution pattern than for the criteria-ideation pattern. These results led the researchers to suggest that patterns involving the suspension of evaluation while ideas are being produced (as, for example, in "brain storming") may tend to produce more potential solutions and more good solutions than would a pattern of discussion in which evaluation is combined with the suggestion of solutions.

Simons has taken a different approach to the question of communication patterns as they affect the outcome of problem-saving deliberations.[30] Using large groups (eighteen to thirty-eight members) of personnel attached to state highway departments, Simons established two experimental conditions: (1) a "representative" pattern, wherein group members committed themselves to a position, announced their position publicly, were grouped with individuals of similar commitments, and selected spokesmen to represent their group in problem-solving discussions; and (2) a "participative" pattern, wherein members were not required to commit themselves to a position, groups were composed randomly rather than of members sharing similar positions, individual differences were discussed within these subgroups, and informative reports were made by subgroup representatives before the large group.

Simons compared these two patterns in three identical experiments. With subjects randomly assigned to conditions, the investigator gathered

[30]Herbert W. Simons, "Representative versus Participative Patterns of Deliberation in Large Groups," *Quarterly Journal of Speech* 52 (1966): 164–71.

data on the correctness of individual postexperimental judgments and on the degree of member satisfaction with the pattern in which he participated. Simons found that a significantly greater number of individuals in the participative pattern identified the correct answer than did those in the representative pattern. Additionally, members in the participative pattern evaluated the behavior of the other subgroups more favorably than did members of the representative pattern. Simons suggested that participative patterns may lead to "wiser" solutions and may also have less of a "divisive" effect on large groups in which individuals differ markedly in attitudes toward the appropriate solution to a problem.

Communication Processes and Member Attitudes

That judgments of group members on a given issue tend to converge if members are aware of others' judgments is one of the better-documented conclusions in small-group research. Grove has argued that much of the early experimentation in this area, particularly that conducted by psychologists, involved laboratory studies so structured that the intermember communication, if it was permitted, was so contrived and "unnatural" as to cast doubt upon the generalization of the findings to communication processes.[31] Speech communication researchers have attempted to investigate relationships between group communication and member attitudes and judgments, and their findings both support and modify the early results of studies by psychologists.

Allowing for discussion of opinions after group members ranked artistic pictures, Simpson found that the divergency of opinions on the re-rankings decreased by approximately 27 percent.[32] Studies such as this have led Paulson to conclude that pressures toward conformity in discussion groups are great, and that "independent judgment" is frequently subjugated to these pressures.[33]

For better or worse, attitudes tend to change as a result of discussion. Utterback has conducted several evaluations of attitude change growing out of intercollegiate conferences on publicly salient topics.[34]

31Theodore G. Grove, "Attitude Convergence in Small Groups," *Journal of Communication* 15 (1965): 226–38.

32Ray H. Simpson, "The Effect of Discussion on Intra-Group Divergencies of Judgment," *Quarterly Journal of Speech* 25 (1939): 546–52.

33Stanley F. Paulson, "Pressures Toward Conformity in Group Discussion," *Quarterly Journal of Speech* 44 (1958): 50–55.

34William E. Utterback, "The Influence of Conference on Opinion," *Quarterly Journal of Speech* 36 (1950): 365–70; idem, "Measuring the Outcome of an Intercollegiate Conference," *Journal of Communication* 6 (1956): 33–37.

A number of consistencies in findings emerge from these studies: (1) Individuals tended to shift opinions toward prediscussion majority viewpoints on slightly more than half the issues discussed. (2) Most of the opinion shift came from those who entered the conferences uncommitted. (3) The discussions resulted in totally new positions being accepted by the group almost as frequently as the group's accepting positions adhered to by majorities. Additionally, Utterback has found that students' attitudes changed more from participating in discussions of short, complex problems than from listening to radio panel discussions of these problems.[35]

Additional data relevant to the question of member attitudes as they are affected by group discussion are provided by Simpson.[36] Simpson found that members of small classroom groups, after discussion of questions on the Minnesota Teacher Attitude Inventory, tended to feel more confidence in their answers to the questions, but tended to be more critical of the issues upon which the questions were based.

Common to the preceding studies is an interest in what the "group" does to the individual's attitudes. Seldom is the question reversed to ask what effect the individual who differs from majority opinion has upon that majority. On the basis of prior-obtained measures of attitudes on two social issues, Grove grouped college students into majority/deviant polarizations.[37] There were four members in each of the forty groups. The groups consisted of three pro and one con or three con and one pro with respect to attitudes toward the topic being discussed. Each group underwent one of five treatments which varied the nature of its expression of opinion (publicly or privately expressed), the presence or absence of discussion, and the length of discussion (fifteen or twenty-five minutes). Among the more significant results are the findings that deal with the nature of the attitudinal change resulting from the discussions. Grove found that discussion of the topics produced more convergence of attitudes than did simple statements of where each individual stood on the topic. He also found that the deviants appreciably altered the attitudes of majority members toward convergence and were themselves altered in all treatments where discussion of the topic occurred.

Utterback gathered change of attitude data on 878 discussions in each of which there existed a majority and a minority.[38] Utterback gave

[35]William E. Utterback, "Radio Panel vs. Group Discussion," *Quarterly Journal of Speech* 50 (1964): 374–77.

[36]Ray H. Simpson, "Attitudinal Effects of Small Group Discussion: Shifts on Certainty-Uncertainty and Agreement-Disagreement Continua," *Quarterly Journal of Speech* 46 (1960): 415–18.

[37]Grove, "Attitude Convergence in Small Groups."

[38]William E. Utterback, "Majority Influence and Cogency of Argument in Discussion," *Quarterly Journal of Speech* 48 (1962): 412–14.

the "right" answer to each problem (and presumably the more cogent arguments) to either the majority or minority and found that the sub-groups, armed with the "right" answer, whether majority or minority, were successful in obtaining significant shifts in judgments from the other members of the group. In a tangentially related study Harnack demonstrated that an organized minority of two individuals, armed with a strategy contrived by the experimenter, could obtain significant shifts in opinion from the majority.[39]

The foregoing studies indicate that considerable convergence of attitude might be expected as a result of group communication, that individuals might be expected to be more committed to their positions after discussion, that most of the influence is exerted by majorities, but that minorities might be expected to have appreciable effects upon majority attitudes, that frequently the final position arrived at through discussion is markedly different from either the majority or minority prediscussion positions, and that discussants might be expected to be more critical of the issues forming the bases for their attitudes after having discussed these issues. The following set of studies deals with factors related to the degree of change in attitudes.

Just prior to World War II a series of studies were conducted involving forty-three discussion groups consisting of college students. The average size of these groups was thirteen. A wide range of experimental situations and data-gathering methods were employed, focusing upon the attitudinal change of participants as related to the following factors: initial attitudes, the information a person possesses on a given topic, sex, temperament (normal, manic, and depressive), the number of participations engaged in by a given individual, "mental alertness" test scores, and the nature of the problem discussed. The results of these studies were reported by Robinson.[40] Among the more significant of Robinson's many findings are these:

1. Analysis of individual shifts of men and women demonstrated that men made a larger percentage of large shifts and women a larger percentage of small shifts as a result of group discussion.
2. In groups heterogeneous as to sex, both men and women made a larger percentage of shifts than in homogeneous groups.
3. Men in homogeneous groups made a larger percentage of significant shifts than did women in like groups; in other words, men in men's groups shifted more than did women in women's groups.

[39]Victor Harnack, "A Study of the Effect of an Organized Minority Upon A Discussion Group," *Journal of Communication* 13 (1963): 12–24.
[40]Karl F. Robinson, "An Experimental Study of the Effects of Group Discussion Upon the Social Attitudes of College Students," *Speech Monographs* 8 (1941): 34–57.

4. There was practically no correlation between changes in attitude and the number of participations in discussion.

5. Small shifts of opinion were found to be closely related to abundant information on a question, whereas larger shifts accompanied lack of information.

Utterback[41] focused his attention on factors different from those investigated by Robinson. Both he and Robinson found no relationship between "intelligence" and shift of opinion, but Utterback was more directly concerned with two other factors, type of problem discussed and prediscussion opinions. With eighty-seven groups of college students discussing problems involving business situations, law cases, and problems of personal conduct, Utterback found that fewer individuals shifted opinions on the law problems than on the other two types. Additionally, the shift of opinion of these individuals varied indirectly with prediscussion distance from neutrality. Utterback would add (1) type of problem discussed and (2) prediscussion opinion to those factors previously discovered to be related to attitudinal changes among group members.

Leadership and Group Communication

We will not engage in a comprehensive treatment of research on leadership here because Chapter 6, "Leadership," is devoted to this topic. At this point we will simply provide some illustrative examples of speech communication research on small-group leadership.

One of the basic questions posed in speech communication research on leadership is whether leadership behavior or "style" can affect the outcomes of discussion. A typical research strategy is to train leaders to exhibit differing leadership styles. Frequently, the research compares leadership behavior which is "group-centered" versus that which is "leader-centered." If "group-centered" can be understood to mean that the leader actively encourages the members of the group to assume responsibility for planning, directing, coordinating, and evaluating the group's activity, then "leader-centered" may be understood to imply that the formally designated leader of the group assumes principal responsibility for these functions. Comparisons between these two forms of leader behavior have yielded the following results: (1) Leader-centered leaders are ranked higher than group-centered leaders in terms of the value of their contribution to the group.[42] (2) Group-centered discussions

---

[41]William E. Utterback, "Independent Variables in the Conference Situation," *Quarterly Journal of Speech* 40 (1954): 381–87.

[42]Richard R. Wischmeier, "Group-Centered and Leader-Centered Leadership: An Experimental Study," *Speech Monographs* 22 (1955): 43–48.

are judged to be better than leader-centered discussions, and are rated higher on such things as involvement, cooperativeness, warm or friendly atmosphere, and ease in making contributions.[43] Group-centered discussions seem to produce greater satisfaction with the decision reached, and a higher rate of member interaction.[44]

A study reported by Mortensen indicates that assigned leaders in student discussion groups may not emerge as the perceived leaders or as individuals who actually exercise substantial influence over group activities.[45] Mortensen's findings tentatively suggest, in combination with those of Wischmeier and Storey, that formally designated leaders may not exert much "desirable" influence on the discussion process. Additionally, Barnlund found that peer ratings of participant's "leadership" varied markedly depending upon the nature of the task confronting the group and the membership of the group.[46] Barnlund's findings support the notions that leadership ratings in small groups are likely to vary across situations and that the results of investigations into leadership phenomena are comparable only if the groups investigated are confronted with similar tasks.

Further clarifying the process of emergent leadership, Geier studied student groups throughout an academic quarter.[47] With particular interest in those member characteristics which may lead peers to reject sustained leadership attempts, Geier discovered that being perceived as uninformed, nonparticipating, and extremely rigid leads to peer rejection in the early stage of group development. In a later stage, authoritativeness and offensive verbalization lead to peer rejection.

The research referred to in this chapter is only a portion of what has been conducted on group communication. Our purpose has been to acquaint you, albeit briefly, with some of the questions that have been posed by speech communication researchers, with the general nature of the research conducted, and with some of the conclusions generated by empirical investigations of group communication phenomena. Some of the more important concepts in this chapter will be explicated in greater detail in subsequent chapters. Presently, our concern is that you begin to see group communication phenomena as something other than the random disorder you may have judged group communication to be on the basis of your past experiences.

43Ibid.; Alfred W. Storey, "Responsibility Sharing versus Strong Procedural Leadership," *Central States Speech Journal* 15 (1964): 285–89.

44Storey, "Responsibility Sharing," pp. 285–89.

45Calvin D. Mortensen, "Should the Discussion Group Have an Assigned Leader?" *The Speech Teacher* 15 (1966): 34–41.

46Dean C. Barnlund, "Consistency of Emergent Leadership in Groups with Changing Tasks and Members," *Speech Minographs* 29 (1962): 45–52.

47John G. Geier, "A Trait Approach to the Study of Leadership," *Journal of Communication* 17 (1967): 316–23.

SUMMARY

1. Although communication is one of the most central processes of human activity, the systematic investigation of human communication is a comparatively recent development.

2. Contemporary speech communication research deals mainly with two questions: (1) What happens when people interact in small groups? (2) What group communication variables are associated with more effective or more rewarding communication activities?

3. Observations about group communication can be organized by isolating process variables and labeling them.

4. Group communication processes are somewhat confusing and unpredictable, but they are not totally random nor do they defy systematic explanation.

5. Fisher has identified four phases through which problem-solving groups pass: orientation, conflict, emergence, and reinforcement.

6. When group members rate each other's effectiveness as discussion participants, higher-rated participants differ from lower-rated participants in a number of ways: confidence in their skill as communicators, satisfaction with the process and product of group deliberations, and need for social affiliations and recognition.

7. The nature and source of evaluations confronting groups affect group communication processes.

8. Group communication researchers have focused considerable attention on problem solving in small groups and have consequently formulated several conclusions on the subject:

   A. Group members possessing high levels of reflective thinking ability may be judged more effective group participants, and groups composed of members all of whom score highly on reflective thinking may produce higher-quality decisions. Nevertheless, it does not necessarily follow that a group which collectively follows a reflective thinking pattern will improve the quality of its problem solving.

   B. Many factors are related to outcomes of problem-solving discussions. Among them are: the sex of the participant, the group members' skill in identifying goals and obstacles within the problem situation, and the problem-solving or communication pattern followed by the group.

   C. Most research on factors related to problem-solving discussion focuses on characteristics of the process rather than on characteristics of the participants.

9. Judgments of group members on a given issue tend to converge if members are aware of other group members' judgments—communication between group members affects member attitudes.

10. As the result of many studies on leadership in small groups, researchers have concluded that: leadership style affects the outcomes of discussion; formally designated leaders may not assert much "desirable" influence on discussion processes; the leadership ratings in small groups are likely to vary across situations.

group communication theory

3

OBJECTIVES

After studying this chapter, you should be able to:

Describe the importance of theory development to the speech communication discipline.

Relate some of the small-group theories in the social psychology literature to group communication.

Name some of the concepts and variables that determine communication process in small groups.

Differentiate among message or behavioral variables, perceptual variables, and concepts that characterize the group as a whole.

Identify the concept of "process strategy" and distinguish it from "outcome strategy."

State four implicit theoretical assumptions of group communication which have influenced group communication specialists.

Until recently, group communication specialists expressed little interest in theory. Although many of them knew that good theory is vital to the growth of a discipline, the early teachers of group communication were primarily concerned with application. They sought to discover or develop principles of good discussion, principles that would serve as standards or guidelines for discussion group teachers, trainers, or members who wanted to improve discussion skills.

Concern about theory increased when group communication specialists began to view themselves as scholars engaged in inquiry into group communication processes, not merely as teachers interested in improving the discussion skills of their students. Good theory, they recognized, is a necessary step in the development of a scientific area of study and research. Theory gives a discipline direction. It allows an investigator to formulate hypotheses that can be tested and to have a framework for explaining his findings. Furthermore, it enables an individual to integrate data that otherwise might appear to be unrelated. Theory also permits one to extrapolate—to go beyond research data and to speculate about the unknown in a systematic and ultimately verifiable way. Since an awareness of theory is essential to the growth of an area of inquiry, the present chapter explores the current status of theory development in group communication.

Because there are relatively few speech communication theories that deal in a comprehensive way with the special concerns of the group communication specialist, group communication scholars and teachers have turned to some of the social psychological theories of small-group behavior in their search for hypotheses and lecture material. The first section of this chapter discusses a number of these theories. The second section identifies the concepts and variables that may ultimately become the ingredients of a theory or theories of group communication. And finally, the chapter sets forth some of the theoretical assumptions that seem to have implicitly guided group communication research in the speech communication discipline.

Social Psychological Theories

A number of theories of small-group behavior have been developed, and many of them are helpful in understanding small-group phenomena. Since the student of group communication is interested in small groups, he should familiarize himself with these theories and their implications. It is important to recognize, however, that group communication is not an area devoted to the study of small groups, per se. Its particular focus is on the communication process in small face-to-face groups. It seeks to understand that process, to explain it, and—given its historic concern with prescription—to formulate principles well grounded in research and theory that will assist individuals and groups in improving their group communication performance. This section of the present chapter examines some of the small-group theories in the social psychological literature that have been helpful to those interested in the communication process in face-to-face groups.

The theories discussed below are not presented in their entirety. Only those aspects of the theories that are of the greatest relevance to the group communication specialist are considered.

HEIDER'S BALANCE THEORY

The general domain of Heider's balance theory[1] is interpersonal relations. Balance theory represents an attempt to explain how individuals who are part of a social structure such as a group are likely to relate to one another. One way a group member can relate, of course, is by communicating overtly. The group member can formulate and transmit verbal messages that others might respond to and he can generate meanings about the messages other group members formulate. But Heider's theory does not deal with this kind of overt communication. Instead, Heider focuses on interpersonal relations that are a function of *attraction*. By attraction, Heider means those cognitive states related to the liking and disliking of other individuals and objects. Hence, Heider's theory deals essentially with what might be referred to as "intrapersonal" communication—that is—it is concerned with certain intrapersonal states that may influence the relationships that exist in a group. Beyond that, the relevance of Heider's balance theory for the group communication scholar is even less direct. Nevertheless, Heider explains the "balance" within a group, and it is conceivable that the group communication specialist may ultimately discover a close relationship between balance and the overt communication behavior of group members.

Heider's balance theory uses the symbol "L" to identify the liking relationship. "L" can refer to many different positive feelings that a group member has about another group member or an object. It can mean that a group member likes another, agrees with another, approves of an act, etc. The symbol "L—" is the negative counterpart of "L." It represents disliking, disapproving, or hating. The symbol "U" represents a unit-forming relationship and is synonymous with "is associated with," "belongs to," "owns," and similar phrases. The opposite of "U" is "U—."

Three other symbols are important to Heider's system. "*p*" refers to person, "*o*" represents some other person or group, and "*x*" refers to an object. Here are some examples of balanced and imbalanced states:

---

[1]Fritz Heider, *The Psychology of Interpersonal Relations* (New York: Wiley, 1956).

State	Symbols	Meaning
Balanced:	*p*L*o*, *o*L*p*	*p* likes *o*, and *o* likes *p*.
	*p*L-*o*, PU-*o*	*p* does not like o and *p* is not a member of the group.
Imbalanced:	*p*L*o*, *o*L-*p*	*p* likes *o* but *o* does not like *p*.
	*p*L*o*, *o*L*x*, *p*L-*x*	*p* likes *o*, *o* likes *x*, but *p* does not like *x*.

Heider's system is a fascinating explanation of group phenomena, and it provides the communication scholar with some valuable ways to look at groups and to deal with intrapersonal events related to the structural dimension of liking. The theory might also be valuable in explaining some overt communication events in groups, even though it does not deal directly with message behavior.

NEWCOMB'S A-B-X SYSTEM

Newcomb's A-B-X system[2] extends Heider's theory of interpersonal relations to the interaction that occurs between members of two-member groups. Newcomb's model includes three elements: A and B, who represent two individuals in interaction, and an object that they communicate about, X. According to Newcomb, the overt communication behavior of A and B can be explained by their need to achieve a state of balance or symmetry with regard to each other and to X. Communication occurs because A must orient himself to B, to X, and to B's orientation to X. Seeking symmetry, A tries to inform himself about B's orientation toward X and this occurs through interaction. Since balance or symmetry is sought, A may be motivated to influence or change B's orientation to X if he discovers an imbalance between them. B, of course, would have a similar motivation with regard to A's orientation. The amount of influence A and B will attempt to exert on each other and the likelihood of their achieving increased symmetry through communicative acts will increase as attraction (Heider's L referred to attraction) and the intensity of the attitude toward X increase.

Newcomb's theory can help the group communication specialist explain and predict the communication behavior of two-member groups. On an intrapersonal level, the theory explains some of the motives and pressures that are likely to generate certain communicative acts, and the theory also describes and explains the acts themselves.

[2]Theodore M. Newcomb, "An Approach to the Study of Communicative Acts," *Psychological Review* 60 (1953): 393–404.

Heider's theory of interpersonal relations deals less directly with small-group communication processes than does Newcomb's A-B-X system. Newcomb's model focuses on the relationships that exist between two individuals in interaction and an object that influences their interaction. A more elaborate small-group theory that includes communication as one of its major components is Festinger's theory of social comparison processes.

FESTINGER'S THEORY OF SOCIAL COMPARISON PROCESSES

In his theory of social comparison processes, Leon Festinger[3] differentiates between physical and social reality. When our opinions, attitudes, and beliefs can readily be validated physically—perhaps by weighing something or measuring its length or height—we are concerned with physical reality, and it may not be necessary for us to communicate much with others. But when our opinions, attitudes, and beliefs are not based on events that are easily measurable and when evidence can be found to support or to contradict them, we are concerned with social reality, and social reality can best be validated by communicating with others who are important to us. Hence, group communication often occurs because of the need individuals have to compare their opinions, attitudes, beliefs, and abilities with those of others.

According to Festinger, the pressure we feel to communicate with other group members about an event increases when we become aware that we are not in agreement concerning that event, when the event increases in importance, and when the cohesiveness of the group increases. As a group member, we are most likely to direct our communications about an event to those who seem most to disagree with us about the event. We are also likely to reduce our communication with those whom we no longer want to view or include as group members. If it appears that a group member to whom we direct our remarks is likely to change, the pressure we feel to communicate with that individual will increase. The amount of change in opinion that our communication will bring about will increase as the pressure on the other person to conform and to remain in the group increases. Festinger suggests, however, that little opinion change will occur among those group members whose opinions about an item "serve important need satisfying functions" or whose opinions are validated by other group memberships.

In addition to conformity pressures, the desire to change our posi-

---

[3]Leon Festinger, "Informal Social Communication," *Psychological Review* 57 (1950): 271–82.

tion (to locomote) in the group's social structure or to change groups will also motivate us to communicate. We may, for example, communicate in order to improve our status in the group or to obtain more acceptance from the other group members. According to Festinger, we are likely to direct our communications to those in the social structure to whom we wish to be closer. Our emotional state is another factor that may encourage us to communicate. Feelings of anger, hostility, euphoria, and the like are hard to contain. Festinger points out, however, that the communication of feelings is consumatory rather than instrumental. Consumatory communication is cathartic. Instrumental communication is associated with task accomplishment.

Group members may experience a great deal of cognitive inconsistency if they are confronted with contradictory facts, opinions, and judgments related to the problem at hand. To reduce that dissonance, members may try to avoid or, if necessary, misinterpret dissonant information. They may also look for and generate messages that support their cognitions.

After a decision is made, group members may communicate with each other to obtain information that produces cognitions that are consonant with the decision. They may also reject or avoid messages that are dissonant with the decision. If a group decision goes contrary to the privately held opinions or beliefs of individual group members, the communication behavior of those members may represent attempts on their part to reduct the dissonance or discrepancy between their public and private views.

THIBAUT AND KELLEY:
SOCIAL EXCHANGE THEORY

In their book, *The Social Psychology of Groups*, Thibaut and Kelley[4] focus primarily on the two-member group or dyad. Thibaut and Kelley are convinced that an understanding of the complex behavior of large groups can be obtained by exploring dyadic relationships as thoroughly as possible. Although their explanation of dyadic behavior involves more than a consideration of communication processes in two-member groups, some of Thibaut and Kelley's formulations are directly relevant to the study of group communication.

Thibaut and Kelley's model supports the assumptions made by Homans in his theory of social exchange processes,[5] namely, that human

4John W. Thibaut and Harold H. Kelley, *The Social Psychology of Groups* (New York: Wiley, 1959).
5George C. Homans, *Social Behavior: Its Elementary Forms* (New York: Harcourt, Brace and World, 1961).

interaction involves the exchange of goods and services, and that the responses individuals in interaction elicit from each other involve both rewards and costs. If the rewards are not sufficient or if they are outweighed by the costs, the interaction will either be terminated or the individuals involved will modify their behavior in order to secure the rewards they seek. Among other things, rewards and costs determine who interacts with whom and what the interaction is about. When two individuals enter into interaction they are likely to maintain that interaction until the rewards drop below a satisfactory level or the costs become intolerable. What constitutes rewards or costs for the members of a dyad is determined by the behavioral repertoires of the participants, their personal standards of satisfaction, power, and dependency, and many other factors.

Thibaut and Kelley's theory is important to the group communication scholar because of its emphasis on social interaction and its use of the economic and behavioral concepts of reward and cost to explain group phenomena. Specific communication variables that constitute rewards and costs for group members have yet to be determined.

MORENO: SOCIOMETRIC THEORY

Sociometry refers to a theoretical and methodological approach to groups that was originated by Moreno[6] and further developed by Jennings[7] and others. Essentially it deals with the attractions and repulsions that individuals feel toward one another and with the implications of these feelings for group formation and structure. A sociometric test is often administered to group members to determine the sociometric structure of a group. The test generally includes questions that require group members to rank one another in terms of their task effectiveness and interpersonal attractiveness. An analysis of the test responses provides insight into the various social configurations or structures that the group members have developed.

Although sociometry is not directly concerned with communication, the sociometric structures of a group are no doubt related in some manner to the communication that occurs within the group. It seems reasonable to assume that individuals who are attracted to each other and who rank each other highly are more likely to communicate in a manner that differs from the way in which group members who repel each other communicate. However, the specific relationship that exists

[6]J. L. Moreno, *Who Shall Survive? A New Approach to the Problem of Human Interrelations* (Washington, D.C.: Nervous and Mental Disease Publishing Co., 1934).
[7]Helen H. Jennings, *Leadership and Isolation*, 2d ed. (New York: Longmans, Green, 1950).

between group communication and group sociometric structures has yet to be determined.

According to Homans,[8] there are three elements of small-group structure: activity, interaction, and sentiment. Activity consists of the acts group members perform that are related to the group task. In their performance of these acts the group members engage in *interaction*; that is, they exhibit interdependent, mutually responsive behavior. Although Homans includes more than communication in his definition of this element, much of the interaction involves interpersonal communication. The third element of social behavior in small groups is sentiment. Sentiment is similar to Heider's concept of liking and consists of the positive and negative feelings that the group members have for one another.

Activity, interaction, and sentiment are interdependent; an increase or decrease in one has an effect on the others. When all three elements are focused on the group's formal tasks or responsibilities the three constitute what Homans calls the formal system. But groups invariably complicate things. The sentiments of liking and disliking that the group members develop toward one another go far beyond the requirements of the group task and they result in a new set of interactions and activities. The sentiments, activities, and interactions that are not directly associated with the formal task responsibilities of the group represent the group's informal system. Theoretically, the informal (internal) system grows out of the formal (external) system, but they both operate concurrently in most groups.

The element of sentiment is an affective one; like Heider's concept of liking, it can be related to intrapersonal communication. In a sense, it deals with the way group members communicate with themselves about other group members. The element of interaction relates most directly to the concerns of the group communication specialist since a large part of what Homans means by interaction is interpersonal communication. Hence, two of the major elements of Homans's theory are concerned at least partially with group communication processes. Homans's theory has provided group communication researchers with worthwhile, testable hypotheses related to such things as the effects of interaction on sentiments, and it has lent further support to the distinction often made by group communication scholars and teachers between task communication (external system) and process communication (internal system).

8George C. Homans, *The Human Group* (New York: Harcourt, Brace and World, 1950).

Although Homans makes interaction an important element of his system, he does not further differentiate that element in a systematic manner. Bales's work dealing with the analysis of interaction processes, on the other hand, consists almost entirely of the analysis of group interaction. An examination of Bales's system follows.

BALES: INTERACTION PROCESS ANALYSIS

Bales[9] has devoted a significant portion of his scholarly career to the development of an Interaction Process Analysis (IPA) category system for analyzing the overt interaction of group members. His IPA category system is carefully described in the following chapter.

The Bales IPA is an equilibrium system. All of its elements are in balance. There are equal numbers of task categories and social-emotional categories, and both of these general categories are divided equally into positive and negative elements. In addition, research indicates that groups engaging in communicative acts associated with task during one session are likely to "restore their equilibrium" by devoting more time to social-emotional acts the next session, and the reverse is also true. Groups also tend to follow a phase progression over time, moving from an initial emphasis on those communication acts associated with orientation, to those acts associated with evaluation, and, finally, to those associated with control. In a sense, these phases, which occur quite naturally in groups, are similar to the problem-solving phases associated with the reflective thinking process described in Chapter 2 and prescribed by many group communication texts.

Bales, like Homans, differentiates between task behaviors and social-emotional (process) behaviors. But the Bales system is distinctive in that it focuses entirely on the communication acts or overt messages that are generated by the members of face-to-face groups. In the speech communication discipline, Scheidel and Crowell,[10] Leathers,[11] Fischer,[12] Sieburg,[13] and other group communication specialists have developed category systems for analyzing communication acts or messages that occur in a group. The efficacy of these approaches, as opposed to theoretical systems and methods that deal entirely or in part with elements

[9]Robert F. Bales, *Interaction Process Analysis: A Method for the Study of Small Groups* (Cambridge, Mass.: Addison-Wesley, 1950).

[10]Thomas M. Scheidel and Laura Crowell, "Feedback in Small Group Communication," *Quarterly Journal of Speech* 52 (1966): 273–78.

[11]Dale G. Leathers, "Process Disruption and Measurement in Group Communication," *Quarterly Journal of Speech* 55 (1969): 287–300.

[12]Aubrey B. Fisher, " 'Decision Emergence,' Phases in Group Decision-Making," *Speech Monographs* 37 (1970): 53–66.

[13]Evelyn Sieburg, "Dysfunctional Communication and Interpersonal Responsiveness in Small Groups" (Ph.D. diss., University of Denver, 1969).

of the group communication process other than overt messages, is an issue that remains to be resolved. Recent research by Litvin[14] strongly suggests that both message variables and perceptual variables must be considered if we are to develop a comprehensive understanding of the communication process in groups.

Bales[15] has theorized that the division of labor, role distinctions, and authority differences that occur when a group is task-oriented create many interpersonal difficulties that can interfere with group solidarity. These difficulties result in pressure to satisfy the interpersonal needs of the members. Bales's insights are especially important to the group communication specialist because he is often called upon to assist groups that are suffering from the strains created by the contradictory pressures associated with task and interpersonal needs.

Group Communication Phenomena

If group communication is an area of study, research, and application that focuses on the communication process in small groups, what are some of the factors or elements that make up that process? The answer largely depends on which communication model or theory as well as on which observational or data-gathering system one employs. As students of group communication, however, we need not be completely arbitrary about the matter. In recent years speech communication scholars have made serious attempts to develop scientific models of the speech communication process. Some of the concepts associated with these models provide a framework for describing and analyzing small-group communication. Finally, in our search for concepts we can examine the work of social scientists identified with a number of disciplines outside of speech communication; these social scientists have developed theories and conducted research dealing with the interaction of individuals in small face-to-face groups.

GROUP COMMUNICATION
CONCEPTS AND VARIABLES

In this section we will identify important concepts and variables in group communication. To study or discuss a subject such as group

14Joel Litvin, "Perceptual Variables vs. Message Behavior Variables; An Exploratory Investigation of Research Priorities in Speech Communication" (Ph.D. diss., University of Denver, 1973).

15Robert F. Bales, "Adaptive and Integrative Changes as Sources of Strain in Social Systems," in *Small Groups: Studies in Social Interaction*, rev. ed., ed. A. Paul Hare, Edgard F. Borgatta, and Robert F. Bales (New York: Knopf, 1965), pp. 127–31.

communication we must engage in what Kaplan referred to as a "process of conceptualization."[16] That is, terms must be assigned to those things and the relationships between them that we are classifying and analyzing. The terms we use can be referred to as *concepts*. A *variable* is a property or characteristic of something that can exist in degrees.[17] Variables can be measured and we can refer to the amount of a variable that is present in a given situation. If we were constructing a scientific theory of group communication in this chapter, we would, among other things, carefully identify and distinguish between our concepts and variables, and we would also systematically discuss the characteristics and attributes of group communication. But our purpose here is merely to identify and briefly describe the concepts and variables that scholars and researchers in speech communication and the behavioral sciences have associated with the group communication process.

This selection of concepts and variables has been influenced by the categories found in the summaries of the small-group research literature provided by McGrath and Altman,[18] Hare,[19] and others, as well as by the list of variables in speech communication developed by Smith in *Speech Communication: Theory and Models.*[20] It should be stressed, however, that the categories presented here have been selected and organized on the basis of their relevance not primarily to small groups, per se, nor to speech communication, but to *group communication.*

CENTRALITY

It has been stressed that group communication can be differentiated from other areas of study in the speech communication discipline and that the group communication specialist differs from small-group specialists in sociology, psychology, and other disciplines because of the primary emphasis he gives to the group communication process. Hence, variables or concepts that deal specifically with communication phenomena are more *central* to group communication than those that refer to other group characteristics or events. But the question of centrality is complicated by the fact that communication scholars have employed two broad categories of variables in their examination of the communication

---

[16]Abraham Kaplan, *The Conduct of Inquiry* (San Francisco: Chandler, 1964), p. 50.

[17]Robert Dubin, *Theory Building* (New York: The Free Press, 1969), p. 35.

[18]Joseph E. McGrath and Irwin Altman, *Small Group Research* (New York: Holt, Rinehart & Winston, 1966).

[19]A. Paul Hare, *Handbook of Small Group Research* (New York: The Free Press of Glencoe, 1962).

[20]Raymond G. Smith, *Speech Communication: Theory and Models* (New York: Harper & Row, 1970).

process, without, in most cases, adequately differentiating between the two or setting forth a rationale for using either category. One category consists of message or behavioral variables and the other contains perceptual variables. A third and final category includes communication concepts that characterize the group as a whole.

BEHAVIORAL VARIABLES
IN GROUP COMMUNICATION

From a behavioral point of view, the central variables in group communication are those that describe the messages that the group members generate and respond to in their interaction with one another. The importance of message variables was stressed by participants in the New Orleans Conference on Research and Instructional Development in Speech-Communication:

> Research in speech-communication focuses on the ways in which messages link participants during interactions. Emphasis is on the behavioral antecedents and consequences of messages and their variations, as well as on the ways that messages interact with communication participants to produce behavioral outcomes.[21]

Message variables in group communication consist of the words as well as the nonvocal gestures and facial expressions that group members use in their interaction with one another. These messages can be described and analyzed in a variety of ways. They can be classified as verbal or nonverbal, intentional or unintentional, or as instrumental or consummatory. They can be rated in terms of intensity, length, rate, abstractness, and along scores of other dimensions. But regardless of how messages are classified or rated, group communication theories will probably take them into consideration.

Group communication theories are likely to distinguish between task messages and process messages, if only because the validity of the distinction has been supported by a great deal of empirical research and small-group theory. On a task level messages are likely to be important elements of theories dealing with idea development in groups and with group decision making and problem solving. Messages are also important elements of theories or those aspects of theories that attempt to explain influence processes in groups and attitude changes on the part of group members.

On a socioemotional or process level, theoretical systems will be

---

[21]Robert F. Kibler and Larry L. Barker, *Conceptual Frontiers in Speech Communication* (New York: Speech Association of America, 1969), p. 33.

developed that will attempt to identify and explain message behavior that reflects the interpersonal concerns and needs of group members. Many of these systems will relate process messages to task messages because of the traditional interest group communication scholars have had in group problem solving and decision making.

The "language" components of messages might be included conceptually in a theory of group communication. Vividness, grammar, unity, and coherence are just some of the language characteristics that could be considered. The vocal characteristics of messages—their quality, pitch, and rhythm, for example—could also be explored.

PERCEPTUAL AND MEMBER VARIABLES IN GROUP COMMUNICATION

Behavioral variables consist of the behaviors group members actually engage in as they interact with one another. They include the things members say to each other and the gestures they use. But the communication process in a small group obviously involves much more than overt communicative acts. Depending upon the internal or perceptual states of the participants, the same words or gestures might mean many different things to group members. Consequently, perceptual variables must be taken into consideration if one is to more fully understand the group communication process.

The perceptual variables, that is, the internal or perceptual states of group members, that are of central concern to the group communication specialist are those that are most directly associated with the communication process. They include the beliefs and attitudes of the group members regarding their own communication behavior, as well as their attitudes toward the communication behavior of other group members and of the group as a whole. They might also involve the members' anxiety about what they or others are communicating, as well as the satisfaction or pleasure they may feel about these same events. Member characteristics of a general or persistent nature such as rigidity or introversion would be less central to group communication than those internal states that are a direct consequence of the group interaction.

Additional perceptual variables associated with group communication are those that are related to the values, ideology, belief system, or assumptions about the communication process that influence the members when they interact with one another. These may include individual or group commitments to democratic procedures, to authenticity and leveling, to particular social, economic, political, or religious creeds, and to certain communication methods or styles.

Potential member variables that are directly related to communication include such communicator characteristics as voice quality, speaking rate, participation level, directness, and the like. On an intrapersonal communication level such factors as the group member's beliefs, reflective thinking skills, open-mindedness, authoritarianism, critical thinking ability, and self-concept as a speaker or group communicator might be considered. The member's awareness of or sensitivity to the communication needs of the other group members, the member's listening skill, ability to understanding the messages of others, and awareness of the communication needs of the group, or the extent to which a member regulates the communication activities of the group with regard to problem-solving, feeling expression, and idea development could all be conceptualized. The group member's honesty as a communicator, tendency to self disclose, to level, to withhold information, to exhibit trust, and similar characteristics often associated with effective human relations might also be included as group member variables in a theory of group communication.

GROUP CHARACTERISTICS

The final category of concepts that might be included in a theory of group communication includes those phenomena of a relational nature than can only be perceived or measured on a group level. Interpersonal feedback, group interaction rate, group phases, group norms, group atmosphere or climate, interpersonal conflict, and leadership distribution are just some of the group characteristics that might be part of a theory of group communication.

SELECTION OF CONCEPTS

An exploration of the communication process in a small face-to-face group can be conducted from a variety of vantage points, and the exploration can have a number of different purposes. The group communication variables you or any other observer may wish to examine or discuss will, of necessity, be a reflection of your interests, frame of reference, theoretical framework, and goals. And since it is not possible to observe or talk about all of the characteristics of a phenomenon at the same time, any particular examination of the group communication process will be somewhat arbitrary and will focus on some aspects of the process and exclude or ignore other aspects of it. Furthermore, the same or similar communication events could be analyzed one way at one time and another way the next. Hence, the concepts identified in this section should be viewed not as a list of mutually exclusive characteristics of the group communication process, but as alternative ways of viewing and describing the interaction of individuals in small face-to-face groups. For the most part, the various foci complement one another, since they consist of different strategies for describing and analyzing the same events. The relative value of various conceptual schemes and observational approaches will be determined, ultimately, by research and theoretical developments in the group communication area.

In this section we have identified concepts that might be included in theories of group communication. But we have not formulated laws or propositions, and we have not taken any other steps generally associated with theory construction. Our failure to do so is deliberate. The purpose of this book is not to present a theory of group communication. Nevertheless, over the years, group communication specialists have been influenced by an implicit theory of group communication. The assumptions of that theory are set forth in the next and final section of this chapter.

Implicit Theory in Speech Communication
Perspective on Groups

Any field of study in the social or behavioral sciences is likely to operate from a variety of theoretical points of view. Some of these points of view take the form of relatively consistent assumptions about the phenomena under investigation. Other points of view are represented by formalized theories; that is, sets of hypotheses and propositions which form deductive systems, with some hypotheses and propositions serving as premises from which other hypotheses and propositions are logically derived. The usual course of events is for a field of study to move from theoretical assumptions toward more and more highly formalized theories. The theoretical assumptions associated with the field of study may be inferred from the work of scholars involved in it—even though the theoretical assumptions may have not yet been formalized into a coherent system of interlocking hypotheses and propositions.

The speech communication perspective on groups is, in our judgment, currently in an intermediate stage of theory construction. First, there are a number of theoretical assumptions that apparently guide the work of speech communication scholars interested in group communication phenomena. Second, there are a number of specific hypotheses and propositions that have been formally stated and tested: for example, that individuals scoring high on reflective thinking ability are likely to be evaluated as more effective group communication participants by other group members with whom such high scorers have interacted. Third, the hypotheses tested by speech communication scholars have not yet been arranged to form a unified formal theory of group communication. Given these circumstances, you should be aware of at least some of the theoretical assumptions underlying much of the work that speech communication scholars have done on group communication, even though these assumptions have not yet been formalized into a theory of group communication. The following, then, are what we believe to be some of the major implicit theoretical assumptions in the speech communication perspective on groups.

I. Group communication may be seen as a process through which judgments are formulated and expressed. This is not to say that groups meet only to solve problems, make decisions, or formulate judgments. Our theory-building strategies rarely enable us to characterize a domain (the set of phenomena to be explained) in terms of every conceivable manifestation of the phenomenon. So we must readily admit that groups may meet for a variety of purposes, including purposes which are primarily oriented toward things other than the formulation and expression of judgment. There is, however, an implicit assumption in the speech communication perspective that implies that many, if not most, groups are concerned predominantly with arriving at decisions, solving problems, or formulating judgments. This assumption, that group communication may be characterized as a process through which judgments are formulated and expressed, simply focuses our attention on certain aspects of group communication and certain properties of groups. As we indicated in our review of speech communication research on groups, the predominant focus among speech communication scholars is reflected in our concern for understanding problem solving, decision making, and judgment processes as they occur in group communication.

II. Judgments are formulated and expressed in group communication through a process which consists of consistently discernible parts. A. Identifying end states. Groups are frequently characterized in terms of purpose, task, or goal. These end states, however ill-defined, provide initial orientation for group members and may even be said to give a group its initial identity. A given end state may be externally prescribed; that is, the group may be assigned a particular task, goal, or purpose by some person or agency outside the group. Indeed, the group may have been formed expressly for the attainment of some end state dictated by an external individual or agent. Or the group may be a voluntary association of individuals who have collected themselves and oriented themselves around a particular goal, task, or purpose. The group may be an ongoing group that frequently confronts, or is confronted by, a variety of tasks, purposes, and goals at various points in its history.

Nonetheless, a consistent assumption of speech communication scholars investigating communication phenomena is that group communication may be characterized as a process through which end states are achieved.

B. Identifying issues related to end states. To solve problems, make decisions, and formulate judgments, all relevant factors and appropriate questions must first be identified. The adequacy of a judgment is assumed to be systematically related to the number and range of relevant issues considered before arriving at the judgment. For example, consider a committee of faculty and students that is meeting to evaluate and develop suggestions for a revision of undergraduate degree requirements. To the extent that a sufficiently wide range of relevant factors and issues are taken into account in arriving at the judgments, then these judgments may be considered adequate. Further, if these judgments are subsequently explained to others who are not involved in the group communication process resulting in the judgments, then the explanation in defense of these judgments will inevitably fall back to the issues and factors taken into account in arriving at the judgments. To put it simply, if I arrive at a decision with respect to problem X, and you ask me a number of questions, and I respond to each question by saying "I didn't think about that," or "I didn't consider that," then you may reasonably conclude that my decision was inadequate.

The relationship between the identification of issues and the adequacy of a judgment is represented by Figure 3–1. The implicit assumption is that the adequacy of a decision increases sharply as more issues bearing on the decision are considered. Then, as the number of relevant

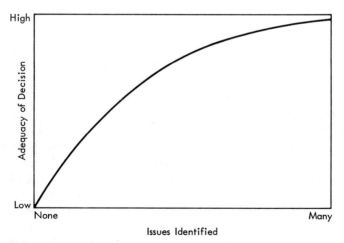

FIGURE 3–1 Hypothesized relationship between issue identification and adequacy of decision.

issues considered continues to increase, the adequacy of judgment levels off. A point of diminishing returns is reached when the number of relevant issues considered begins to exceed the capacity of the group to recall and relate issues to the specific problem, task, or purpose under consideration.

C. Pooling resources for the resolution of issues. As we indicated in our review of speech communication research on small groups, one of the conclusions considered "well established" in the first phases of group communication research was that groups are superior to individuals when dealing with problems permitting a wide range of responses. Generally, group judgments tend to be more adequate than individual judgments in situations where a wide range of issues and factors must be considered in formulating a judgment. Put simply, a group presumably has at its disposal all of the resources (experiences, knowledge, interpretative skills) possessed by all members of the group. Just as problem-solving accuracy is related to the identification of issues relevant to the problem, the resolution of issues, once identified, depends upon the availability of facts, information, experiences, and interpretative and analytic skills which can be brought to bear on the issues. Thus, another implicit theoretical assumption is that the pooling of member resources is more likely to result in adequate resolution of issues than would be the case for any given member of the group. Of course, a more basic assumption is that the resources possessed by group members do not overlap a great deal. To the extent that all members share essentially the same opinions, are in command of essentially the same facts, and have had essentially the same kinds of experience, the adequacy of issue resolution is decreased. Thus, Figure 3–2 represents the assumed relationship between nonduplicated resources and the adequacy of issue resolution.

D. Making judgments explicit. Group communications serves the basic function of making judgments explicit. If you recall our earlier discussion of basic group communication process research, and if you add to that research your own experiences with group communication, you may agree that judgments characteristically are expressed tentatively in the initial phases of group communication. The initial tentative expression of judgment, the reinforcement and agreement obtained for some judgments, the disagreement with and withdrawal of other judgments, and the eventual emergence of a group or collective judgment are usual parts of the process of making judgments explicit.

III. An implicit theoretical assumption which will be dealt with in much greater detail in the next chapter is that group communication performs for individuals what has been referred to as the "linking" function of speech communication. One of the basic functions of speech

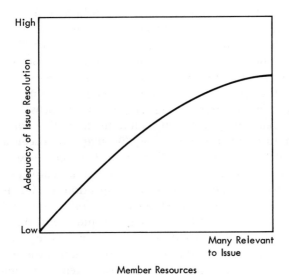

FIGURE 3–2 Hypothesized relationship between member resources and adequacy of issue resolution.

communication is the development and maintenance of linkages between the individual and his environment. This linking function, as it relates to group communication, is the basic process through which individuals establish connections for themselves at two levels, the personal and the purpose level.

Consider first the personal level. In the next chapter we will support the general notion that one basic inclination for most individuals is the search for acknowledgment and confirmation. Most of us wish to be attended to, responded to directly, and confirmed in terms of our inherent value as individuals and the worth of our ideas. A communicative act in a group is first and foremost a personal act. It is a disclosure of self, even if such a disclosure comes in the form of what I know, what I have experienced, or what I believe. If an individual's communicative act is ignored, the individual is left with some doubt, however transient and ill-defined, concerning his value as a person or the worth of his verbal offering. If his communicative act is treated tangentially but dismissed, the doubt remains, although perhaps to a lesser degree. Our contention is that if an individual's communicative act is acknowledged, responded to directly, and interpreted as having something to do with the purpose at hand, then the individual has established a connection at the personal level.

With respect to the purpose level, to the extent that an individual perceives his communicative acts as having *consequences*, as somehow affecting the judgments of others and ultimately the collective judgment, the individual has established connections at the purpose level. As we shall see in the next chapter, in our discussion of Sieburg's work,[22] these notions of acknowledgment and confirmation are central concepts in distinguishing effective from ineffective communication processes.

IV. Implicit in the speech communication perspective on groups are two related strategies. *Process strategy* represents a focus on (1) explaining (2) what is happening in group communication. The *outcome strategy* represents a focus on (1) predicting (2) what will occur as a result of group communication. The distinction between these two strategies is not absolute; rather, they represent different emphases in theory building and research. When speech communication scholars have focused on outcomes, they have oriented themselves primarily around three questions: (1) Under what conditions are group judgments likely to be more adequate? (2) Under what conditions are sentiments (e.g., interpersonal attraction, attraction for the group, satisfaction with group deliberation) formed and maintained? (3) To what extent, and under what conditions, are member attitudes affected by group communication?

When speech communication scholars have focused on process, they have frequently oriented themselves toward questions dealing with how judgments are expressed and modified, how feedback operates in response to communicative acts, and how certain classes of communication behavior affect subsequent events in groups, or the behavior of other group members, or simply the frequency of types of message sending and receiving behavior in groups. Again, the distinction between process and outcome orientations is not absolute. However, to the extent that such a distinction can be made, the remainder of this book follows primarily, although not exclusively, a process strategy. This chapter has reviewed some of the more widely accepted theoretical explanations of group communication processes. The next chapter develops some guidelines for observing what happens during group communication.

SUMMARY

1. Relatively few comprehensive theories of speech communication have been formulated that deal with the special concerns of group communication specialists.

2. Theory is necessary to a discipline: it provides direction and a frame-

---

[22] Sieburg, "Dysfunctional Communication."

work for the formulation and testing of hypotheses; it enables the researcher to integrate seemingly unrelated data; and it allows speculation about the unknown in a systematic way.

3. Several theories from social psychology are helpful in explaining and predicting group communication behavior.

A. Heider's balance theory is concerned with certain intrapersonal states that may influence the relationships that exist in a group, especially those related to liking; the theory does not deal with message behavior but there may be a relationship between Heider's "balance" and overt communication behavior.

B. Newcomb's A-B-X system focuses on the relationships that exist between two individuals (A and B) in interaction and an object (X) that influences their interaction.

C. Festinger's theory of social comparison processes is based on the premise that group communication often occurs because of the need individuals have to compare and evaluate their perceptions of "social reality" (i.e., opinions, attitudes, belief). The theory attempts to explain why communication increases or decreases between group members.

D. The Thibaut and Kelley social exchange theory focuses on the two-member group, or dyad, and uses the economic and behavioral concepts of reward and cost to explain group interaction.

E. Moreno's sociometric theory deals with the attractions and repulsions that individuals feel toward one another and the implications of such feelings for group formation and structure and possibly for communication.

F. Homans's internal and external system recognizes three independent elements of small-group structure: activity, interaction, and sentiment. Interaction (which relates to interpersonal communication) and sentiment (which relates to intrapersonal communication) are of most interest to the communication specialist. Homans's theory supports the distinction group communication makes between task communication (external system) and process communication (internal system).

G. Bales's interaction process analysis is a category system for analyzing the overt interaction of group members; it provides useful insights into the strains caused by the contradictory pressures of task and interpersonal needs.

4. Concepts and variables related to group communication fall into three major categories:

A. Behavioral variables—the things members say to each other and the gestures, expressions, tone of voice, etc. they use; the overt communication acts.

B. Perceptual variables—the internal states of members such as beliefs and attitudes, anxiety and pleasure, and rigidity and introversion; and member variables—such things as voice quality, open-mindedness, self-concept, sensitivity, and tendency to self-disclose.

C. Group characteristics—such things as interpersonal feedback, group interaction rate, phases, norms, climate, and leadership.

5. Group communication specialists have been influenced by an implicit theory of group communication which has at least four basic assumptions. These assumptions have not yet been formalized into a formal theory of group communication.

6. Process strategy focuses on explaining what is happening in group communication, while outcome strategy focuses on predicting what will occur as a result of group communication. (Group communication as discussed in this book focuses mainly on process strategy.)

discussion:
the
speech communication
tradition

OBJECTIVES

After studying this chapter, you should be able to:

Trace the history of group communication and identify the ideas and concepts with which group communication specialists were concerned in the past.

Explain the historical base upon which the present field of group communication has been built.

Discuss the limitations of traditional discussion approaches.

Define and use accurately the vocabulary or taxonomy of discussion and group communication as it appears in this chapter.

If you consider it a virtue to "do your own thing," you might be somewhat disturbed about the implications of a textbook such as ours that focuses on the communication process in small groups. Groups occasionally subject their members to strong and sometimes irresistible pressure to conform, and to the extent that a group communication text encourages more group participation, its publication could be interpreted by some as another step toward the loss of individuality in our society.

Although we thoroughly reject the view of some right-wing extremists who claim that group researchers and practitioners are engaged in a communist-inspired conspiracy against individualism in our society, we recognize that the issue of individuality versus group conformity is a serious one. It is an issue that speech communication specialists have addressed and argued about ever since the development of discussion as an area of study and application in the 1930s. The legitimacy of the issue is supported both by the research that has been done on group conformity and by the pressures to conform that most of us have experienced as members of groups. But the fact that groups often influence the beliefs, attitudes, and opinions of their members does not imply that group communication specialists are "antiindividualistic." Quite the contrary. The study of group communication, we are convinced, grew out of the attempt on the part of early discussion scholars to help individuals solve problems more effectively in groups without sacrificing their individuality.

Individuality versus group conformity is just one of the many issues on which group communication specialists have focused. This chapter examines the various issues, concepts, concerns, and approaches that are part of the group communication tradition. It describes group communication as it has been and as it still is being written about and taught by many speech communication teachers. It acquaints us with our field so that we can profit from the wisdom of the past and better understand contemporary developments and concerns.

Some interest in group communication as an area of study, research, and application in speech communication has existed ever since the establishment of modern speech departments over fifty years ago. Research in group communication was conducted by speech communication scholars throughout the 1920s and 1930s.[1] But it was not until the publication in 1939 of *Discussion in Human Affairs*, by McBurney and Hance,[2] that group communication established itself as a vital and expanding part of the speech communication curriculum. The area was not called group communication back then. Until fairly recently, the general area of concern was referred to as discussion, and today it is still given that label by many people.

Discussion in Human Affairs was not the first text devoted in whole or in part to discussion. It was, however, one of the first books to provide a philosophical rationale for the area that was compatible with the interests and concerns of many others in the speech communication discipline. McBurney and Hance pointed out that unlike persuasion and argumentation, which are concerned with advocacy, discussion is devoted to inquiry and can be identified with the scientific method.

---

[1]Milton Dickens and Marguerite Hefferman, "Experimental Research in Group Discussion," *Quarterly Journal of Speech* 35 (1949): 23–29.

[2]James H. McBurney and Kenneth G. Hance, *Discussion in Human Affairs* (New York: Harper & Brothers, 1939).

McBurney and Hance also described a procedure based on Dewey's steps of reflective thinking that gave students, teachers, and future discussion textbook writers a system for teaching and improving small-group problem-solving discussions.

The Past Purpose of Discussion

Until recently, discussion has been viewed by most discussion textbook writers and teachers as an area devoted to improving the performance of discussants and discussion groups. This emphasis on skill development did not apply to all groups. It was restricted largely to "task-oriented" groups, to groups engaged in problem solving or decision making where the group's goals were relatively clear and the discussion group had an explicit purpose. Groups concerned with the emotional needs of their individual members, such as therapy groups, were thought of largely as outside the boundaries of "discussion." In their early text, Wagner and Arnold stated explicitly that they were "concerned exclusively with problem-solving discussion."[3] More recently, Bormann described discussion as "serious and systematic talk about a clearly specific topic. Discussion is task-oriented. People engaged in discussion have a common purpose and are striving for common goals."[4]

In addition to being limited to certain kinds of groups, the emphasis on skill development was also restricted to certain kinds of group interaction. The primary focus was on task-oriented interaction, on those communication acts that dealt directly or indirectly with the problem at hand. For the most part, comments that reflected the psychological needs of the group members or the maintenance needs of the group were not given serious attention. Nontask communications were not completely ignored, but if considered at all, they were usually dealt with in terms of their relationship to the group task.

Crucial to an understanding of discussion as it was and still is traditionally taught and written about by many speech communication specialists is the awareness that it emphasized skill development and not systematic inquiry into the nature of the discussion process. We are not suggesting that an understanding of the discussion process itself was considered unimportant. Quite the contrary, understanding was felt to be essential to skill development. Many textbook writers agreed that the purpose of discussion as an area of study was to help students better

[3]Russell H. Wagner and Carroll C. Arnold, *Handbook of Group Discussion* (Boston: Houghton Mifflin, 1950), p. 6.

[4]Ernest G. Bormann, *Discussion and Group Methods* (New York: Harper & Row, 1969), p. 4.

understand the discussion process and to help them improve their discussion attitudes and skills. But the understanding sought by the authors of a book or the teachers of a course devoted to skill training is likely to differ considerably from the content of a book or a course that is devoted as much to systematic inquiry as it is to skill improvement.

If discussion had been viewed as an area of inquiry, discussion texts and courses in the past would have been concerned with a variety of matters that, for the most part, they ignored. For example, they would have examined or developed theories of group interaction. They would have described different ways of measuring the discussion process. They would have synthesized the findings of researchers who have studied small discussion groups. Many of these matters and more, of course, were considered on a limited basis, especially by some of the more recent writers of discussion texts. But most of the earlier discussion texts and courses focused on improving the skills of discussants and enhancing the performance of problem-solving discussion groups, and not on the development of discussion as an area of inquiry and scholarship.

The following synthesis of a number of basic discussion texts is designed to provide the reader with a comprehensive picture of the traditional approaches to discussion that have been followed by speech communication teachers and scholars.

Definition:
The Nature of Discussion

Most discussion texts until now have been concerned with helping discussants and discussion groups improve their discussion behavior. They have attempted to achieve this goal by, among other things: (1) discussing the nature of discussion, its philosophic rationale, and its purposes; (2) providing the reader with information about discussion groups and insights into group behavior; (3) identifying principles of good discussion; and (4) prescribing rules or suggesting procedures that are likely to improve the quality of discussion.

GROUP SIZE

All of the major discussion texts agree that discussion involves a small number of individuals who interact with one another in a face-to-face group for one session or more. Most texts suggest that the group can be as small as two, but Utterback[5] considers five to be the smallest number.

---

[5]William E. Utterback, *Group Thinking and Conference Leadership* (New York: Holt, Rinehart & Winston, 1964), p. 4.

All suggest that the group should be relatively small. Twenty group members are generally considered the upper limit, but Sattler and Miller[6] mention thirty to forty as a maximum.

INTERACTION

The texts also agree that discussion takes place through oral discourse. The interaction is continuous, says Brilhart,[7] and, according to Howell and Smith, it involves "both purposive and accidental transmission of meanings from one mind to another."[8] The interaction is also described by some authors as free and open.[9]

PURPOSE

Discussion is viewed by most authors of discussion texts as deliberate and purposeful. The participants, according to Crowell,[10] have a common goal. Discussion is generally viewed as a problem-solving or decision-making activity and both terms are used interchangeably in the literature. Howell and Smith[11] claim that discussion arises out of our need to solve problems, and Bormann states that discussants communicate "to fulfill a common purpose and achieve a group goal."[12] The specific goals are identified by many texts as enlightenment and understanding or as action. There is relatively common agreement that cooperation among the discussion group members is an essential ingredient of discussion.

Gulley[13] points out that discussion is systematic. Others stress the importance or value of being systematic, but they do not include that factor in their definition of discussion. Most texts state that discussion usually occurs under the direction of a leader.

Traditionally, then, discussion has been viewed as a problem-solving activity, as a process involving two or more people communicating orally with each other in a small face-to-face group. The participants have a common purpose. They are seeking understanding, policy deter-

---

6William M. Sattler and N. Edd Miller, *Discussion and Conference* (Englewood Cliffs, N.J.: Prentice-Hall, 1968), p. 23.

7John K. Brilhart, *Effective Group Discussion* (Dubuque, Iowa: William C. Brown, 1967), p. 2.

8William S. Howell and Donald K. Smith, *Discussion* (New York: Macmillan, 1956), p. 192.

9Sattler and Miller, *Discussion and Conference*, p. 23.

10Laura Crowell, *Discussion: Method of Democracy* (Chicago: Scott, Foresman, 1963), pp. 40–41.

11Howell and Smith, *Discussion*, p. 3.

12Bormann, *Discussion and Group Methods*, p. 3.

13Halbert E. Gulley, *Discussion, Conference, and Group Process* (New York: Henry Holt, 1960), p. 5.

mination, or action. The interaction ought to be systematic, and it is likely to occur under the direction of a leader.

The Characteristics of Discussion

A number of terms are used in the literature to characterize discussion. Discussion, according to Barnlund and Haiman,[14] is a dynamic, ever-changing process. It's a form of discourse, Howell and Smith[15] assert, that is essential to our lives. Cartright and Hinds expand on this by pointing out that it is a necessary ingredient in all cooperative endeavors. Cartright and Hinds also claim that discussion is based upon a faith in human nature, in our ability to discover truth through open and free interaction, and in majority rule.[16]

RATIONALE

McBurney and Hance[17] developed a rationale for discussion by considering four basic relations. The first is the relationship between inquiry and advocacy. Discussion, they point out, is identified with the scientific method and involves a systematic and open-minded examination of a problem. Howell and Smith[18] also differentiate discussion from advocacy. Wagner and Arnold[19] refer to discussion as the empirical method, since it involves the adaptation of the scientific method for solving social, economic, and political activities.

The alternative to free and open inquiry is advocacy. Advocacy is associated with the methods of persuasion and debate, and it is most likely to be used by individuals who have completed their inquiry into a problem and have made up their minds. At this point, they are less interested in further inquiry than they are in persuading others to accept their own findings and conclusions. Gulley[20] points out that the two processes complement one another. After a period of advocacy, individuals may want to engage in further discussion or inquiry.

A second relationship that McBurney and Hance[21] consider involves reflective thinking and intentional reasoning. They identify the

---

14Dean C. Barnlund and Franklyn S. Haiman, *The Dynamics of Discussion* (Boston: Houghton Mifflin, 1960), p. xvi.

15Howell and Smith, *Discussion*, p. 3.

16Rupert L. Cartright and George L. Hinds, *Creative Discussion* (New York: Macmillan, 1959), pp. 3–6.

17McBurney and Hance, *Discussion in Human Affairs*, pp. 3–7.

18Howell and Smith, *Discussion*, pp. 7–8.

19Wagner and Arnold, *Handbook of Group Discussion*, p. 8.

20Gulley, *Discussion, Conference, and Group Process*, pp. 9–11.

21McBurney and Hance, *Discussion in Human Affairs*, p. 4.

reflective thinking process as developed by John Dewey in his book, *How We Think*,[22] with the process of inquiry. The reflective thinker is not interested in supporting certain points of view at the expense of others. He is willing to search and discover the truth wherever and whatever it may be. Discussion, they claim, represents an attempt on the part of a group to think together reflectively, and they differentiate such a process from intentional reasoning, which consists of the development of a line of reasoning designed to support certain conclusions that have already been reached.

Third, McBurney and Hance[23] distinguish between criticism and propaganda. The propagandist tries to convince others to accept a predetermined set of conclusions. The critic is willing to critically examine events and to reserve judgments until a reasonable amount of data has been carefully considered. Cartright and Hinds,[24] as well as McBurney and Hance, identify discussion with the process of criticism.

Finally, McBurney and Hance[25] associate discussion with cooperation as opposed to competition. It has been pointed out that a number of texts include a reference to cooperation in their definition of discussion. The processes of inquiry, constructive reasoning, and criticism require cooperation rather than competition. Cartright and Hinds[26] make a similar point when they distinguish between consent and consensus as opposed to coercion and conflict.

Discussion and Democracy

Utterback[27] claims that discussion is an essential part of the democratic process because democracy can be defined as government by talk. Discussion also has been identified with democracy by many other writers of discussion texts. The two terms are practically synonymous to some, and for many compelling reasons. For example, one might operationally define democracy as that process whereby individuals who are to be affected by a decision participate in the making of it. This operational definition of democracy is also a common definition of the discussion process.[28] Brilhart[29] writes that discussion and democracy are like the two sides of a coin. Democracy cannot function without discussion.

The relationship between democracy and discussion was important

22John Dewey, *How We Think* (Boston: Heath, 1910).
23McBurney and Hance, *Discussion in Human Affairs*, pp. 5–7.
24 Cartright and Hinds, *Creative Discussion*, p. 7.
25McBurney and Hance, *Discussion in Human Affairs*, p. 7.
26Cartright and Hinds, *Creative Discussion*, p. 8.
27Utterback, *Group Thinking and Conference Leadership*, p. 8.
28Barnlund and Haiman, *The Dynamics of Discussion*, p. 5
29Brilhart, *Effective Group Discussion*, pp. 3–4.

enough to Crowell for her to include a reference to the relationship in the title of her text, *Discussion: Method of Democracy*. Persuasion and debate are also methods of democracy that interest speech communication teachers and scholars, but discussion tends to be viewed as the most democratic of the three. McBurney and Hance[30] stress the importance of all three methods, but they see debate and persuasion as essentially back-up procedures to be used when discussion fails.

Discussion is identified with democracy because it provides a method for democratic participation. In addition to this, democracy and discussion represent a commitment to similar values. Both are based on a belief in the dignity and worth of every person[31] and in the right of every individual, regardless of his social or economic status, to contribute freely and equally to the decision-making process. Both stress the importance of cooperation, teamwork, respect and concern for others, and "self-government."[32,33] And both can only survive, Barnlund and Haiman[34] point out, if enough resistance can be mustered to such hostile factors and forces as apathy, secrecy, censorship, and centrality of power.

The Growth of Discussion

The use of group discussion in decision making or problem solving has increased considerably since the turn of the century. The number of college courses in discussion and group communication has also expanded rapidly during this same period. Many factors are no doubt responsible for these developments, and various discussion texts have attempted to identify them. Historical, political, social, and personal events have been cited to explain the growth.

Bormann[35] and Harnack and Fest[36] refer to the urbanization of American life as an important factor in the development of discussion. The shift from an emphasis on individualism and an enthusiasm for agrarian values to urban corporate structures and the need for security, for getting along with others at work, and for "having friends," contributed to the rise of discussion. Urbanization means greater interdependence, greater complexity, and a greater reliance on group decision—fewer instances where the individual can do whatever he pleases.

30McBurney and Hance, *Discussion in Human Affairs*, p. 38.
31Howell and Smith, *Discussion*, p. 12.
32Crowell, *Discussion: Method of Democracy*, pp. 321–23.
33Gulley, *Discussion, Conference, and Group Process*, pp. 1 and 8.
34Barnlund and Haiman, *The Dynamics of Discussion*, pp. 347–72.
35Bormann, *Discussion and Group Methods*, pp. 7–8.
36R. Victor Harnack and Thorrel B. Fest, *Group Discussion: Theory and Technique*, (New York: Meredith, 1964) p. 9.

In addition to "the fall of the individual,"[37] the growth of discussion has been attributed to advances in the scientific method and to the inevitable desire on the part of individuals who were impressed with the efficacy of science in dealing with physical and technical matters to apply scientific methods of human affairs.[38] Among other things, such an application involves the use of a communication method such as discussion that is associated with "scientific inquiry" as opposed to methods identified with advocacy or persuasion.

The increasing pragmatism of higher education[39] with its emphasis on practical insights and skills rather than knowledge for its own sake also encouraged the growth of courses in discussion. And the application of John Dewey's reflective thinking process to discussion provided a systematic way in which discussion could be applied to practical affairs. The reflective thinking process represented a scientific approach to decision making, and the fact that this process could be used by groups further increased the attractiveness of discussion.

It has been pointed out that discussion is seen as a democratic procedure. Hence, interest in discussion and its use are likely to increase as interest in and use of democratic procedures increase. According to Barnlund and Haiman, many factors are responsible for the expansion of democratic processes in this country during the past half century. They include a greater awareness of and concern for the dignity of the individual, a higher average level of education that has resulted in a greater distribution of knowledge, and a greater equalization of economic and physical power.[40] Better-educated and more powerful citizens have more to contribute and are more likely to demand a voice in decision making. These factors have expanded the use of discussion methods in business, education, government, the family, and other institutions and organizations.

Other factors responsible for the growth of discussion might be placed in a category called *"concurrent developments,"* since they include such events as the adult education movement and the growing use of panels and other discussion formats on radio and TV. These concurrent events stimulated the growth of discussion because they too, either directly or indirectly, involved group methods or approaches. The development of college courses in group dynamics, small-group research, and group practices and the entire human relations movement with its emphasis on small-group laboratory learning, T-grouping, encounter, and sensitivity training, had a similar impact on the growth of discussion.

[37]Harnack and Fest, *Group Discussion: Theory and Technique*, p. 9.
[38]Barnlund and Haiman, *The Dynamics of Discussion*, pp. 9–10.
[39]Bormann, *Discussion and Group Methods*, pp. 10–11.
[40]Barnlund and Haiman, *The Dynamics of Discussion*, pp. 6–15.

Perhaps a final factor responsible for the expanded interest in discussion is the deliberate attempt on the part of many individuals who were committed to group approaches to learning and to democratic methods, to promote the use of discussion. If, as Gulley put it, "discussion is one of the fundamental processes of decision-making in a democratic society,"[41] then specialists in discussion and group communication have an obligation to encourage others to use the method and to improve their skill as discussants. This obligation was emphasized by Lee, in *How to Talk with People*, when he responded to some of the events responsible for World War II by stating that "The lesson of our experience is that we must not sit by and expect a faith in democracy to evolve by itself into democratic forms of action."[42] To some extent, then, the growth of discussion can be attributed to the initiative of those discussion specialists in speech communication who had an abiding faith in democratic procedures and who had the determination to do something about it.

Types of Discussion Groups

Most discussion specialists in the past viewed discussion as a goal-directed decision-making activity. Hence, they focused primarily on task-oriented groups whose members were ostensibly, at least, concerned with learning, policy formulation, or action, and not primarily with such matters as personal adjustment and growth, therapy, self-insight, or catharsis. Many discussion texts devoted largely to decision making, however, identified the wide range of purposes for which discussion might be suited, and they also described the many forms and structures discussions could assume. The next section summarizes some of the discussion uses, purposes, forms, and structures that have been identified and described in the literature.

Dimensions and Categories

Discussion groups have been classified along a variety of dimensions, and these different classification systems have resulted in many overlapping sets of categories. Purpose or goal is the most common dimension used to classify discussion groups, and this standard has resulted in categories related to group tasks and categories related to the personal

[41]Gulley, *Discussion, Conference, and Group Process*, p. v.
[42]Irving J. Lee, *How to Talk with People* (New York: Harper & Brothers, 1952), p. 171.

or process needs of group members. In the task area, decision-making or problem-solving discussion groups are commonly identified, although distinctions are often made between task groups that are policy-making and those that implement policies through action.[43,44] Gulley describes action groups as those that have the power to act on their decisions, and he differentiates between action groups and recommendation groups.[45]

In the process area, discussion groups whose primary goal is to satisfy the interpersonal needs of their members have been classified as social[46] or as casual.[47] Those groups that are formed primarily to help their members deal with personal problems of growth, development, and adjustment have been labeled "cathartic" or "therapeutic."[48] Discussion groups that are formed to satisfy the educational goals of their members are generally placed near the middle of the goal continuum and are classified as learning groups.[49]

Another major distinction is made between private discussions that are conducted without onlookers, and public discussions that are designed to enlighten and, in some cases, entertain an audience or a group of observers.[50] Although public versus private, and task versus process distinctions based on goal or purpose are the most common, a number of additional discussion group category systems can be found in the literature. Sattler and Miller, for example, use physical arrangement as a standard and differentiate between very informal, semiformal, and formal groups.[51] Harnack and Fest focus on the circumstances which brought the group members together and differentiate between discussion groups formed casually, voluntarily, and involuntarily.[52] Bormann differentiates between groups on the basis of the uses to which their discussions are put—such as to inform, to stimulate interest, to solve problems, and to stimulate creativity.[53]

Most discussion texts identify a variety of discussion forms or types. These forms represent either different formats for conducting public discussions before an audience or different ways to achieve the learning

43Barnlund and Haiman, *The Dynamics of Discussion*, pp. 26–28.

44Harnack and Fest, *Group Discussion: Theory and Technique*, p. 44.

45Gulley, *Discussion, Conference, and Group Process*, p. 34.

46Harnack and Fest, *Group Discussion: Theory and Technique*, p. 42.

47Barnlund and Haiman, *The Dynamics of Discussion*, pp. 21–23.

48Harnack and Fest, *Group Discussion: Theory and Technique*, pp. 42–43; Cartright and Hinds, *Creative Discussion*, p. 255.

49Sattler and Miller, *Discussion and Conference*, p. 59; Barnlund and Haiman, *The Dynamics of Discussion*, pp. 24–26.

50Gulley, *Discussion, Conference, and Group Process*, pp. 27–28; Wagner and Arnold, *Handbook of Group Discussion*, pp. 165–83; Keltner, *Group Discussion Processes*, (New York: Longmans, Green, 1957) pp. 16–21.

51Sattler and Miller, *Discussion and Conference*, p. 59.

52 Harnack and Fest, *Group Discussion: Theory and Technique*, pp. 47–50.

53Bormann, *Discussion and Group Methods*, pp. 32–34.

or decision-making goals of participants involved in private discussions. Here are some of the more common discussion forms or types that are found in discussion texts, along with a brief explanation of each one.

Panel

A panel discussion generally involves a small group of discussants who talk informally about a particular topic that each participant has carefully explored ahead of time. The panel is usually led by a moderator and the interaction, although spontaneous, is preplanned. Panelists can interrupt each other and the group is free to deviate somewhat from the established topic and format, but enough planning goes into the event to assure the audience and the participants a lively and worthwhile experience.

Symposium

A symposium consists of a series of relatively brief but formal presentations dealing with a central theme or topic. After the formal presentations, the members of the symposium may answer questions from the floor or engage in a panel discussion among themselves.

Forum

Forum generally refers to a period of time that is set aside for audience participation. Members of the audience may express their own points of view, ask questions of each other or a panel, or enter into the general discussion in other ways. Forums are often part of a panel discussion or symposium and are generally handled by a moderator.

Colloquy

A colloquy consists of an "expert" or a group of "experts" who are questioned by members of the audience or perhaps by members of the press. The experts are not briefed on the specific questions that they will be asked, but they are generally aware of the topics that will be covered.

Committee

The word "committee" is generally used to identify a discussion group that has been given a specific task or responsibility by a larger organization or an authority figure.

Conference

When representatives of different groups or organizations get together to discuss common problems, the gathering is sometimes referred to as a conference. Conference is also used to describe a meeting between two individuals at which important matters are discussed.

Case Discussion

Case discussions are usually conducted for instructional purposes. They involve a discussion that centers around a written or orally presented case. The case usually describes a real or hypothetical situation that is related in some way to the material the group is attempting to learn.

Buzz Group

When an audience is broken down into small face-to-face groups and asked to discuss a topic, the groups are sometimes called buzz groups. Buzz groups may be asked to appoint a spokesperson who will inform the entire audience of the conclusions they reach.

Dialogue

When two individuals are asked to discuss a topic with each other in front of an audience, the interaction is referred to as a dialogue.

Round-table

The label round-table can be used to identify a situation where individuals are invited to gather in a circle to discuss an issue or resolve a problem over an extended period of time, while nonparticipants sit around them and observe the interaction.

Discussion Problems

Although a variety of discussion purposes and forms have been recognized and identified by many discussion texts, most texts focus primarily if not entirely on discussions that are deliberate and that focus on a problem-solving or decision-making task. And since rhetorical theory suggests that communicators can handle their tasks most effectively if they first carefully determine what it is they are attempting to achieve, discussion texts have identified the types of problem task-oriented discussion groups are likely to deal with.

Discussion problems ought to be phrased in the form of questions and not as assertions or propositions, according to McBurney and Hance,[54] because discussion is a form of inquiry and a question is more likely to start the discussants off on the correct path. Some questions are more appropriate for discussion than others. A good discussion question, according to Crowell, should be suited to the group purpose and to the time available to the group. It should also be interesting and worthwhile.[55] Wagner and Arnold suggest that it should lend itself to reflective thinking and that it should involve more than two solutions.[56] Harnack and Fest warn that the question should not imply a particular solution and that it should specify whose behavior is subject to change.[57]

Most texts agree that discussion questions fall into three major categories: questions of fact, of value, and of policy. Questions of fact deal with truth and falsity, with the existence of things, with causation, and with the prediction of future events. Questions of value are essentially concerned with appraisal, with the goodness or badness or the rightness or wrongness of individuals, actions, or events. Questions of policy are the most appropriate for discussion and they ask what, if anything, should be done about something. Barnlund and Haiman deviate somewhat from this traditional category system; in addition to problems of "fact or perception" and problems of "attitude and feeling" (similar in some ways to value questions), they identify problems of diagnosis and understanding that involve the interpretation of events.[58]

The Reflective Thinking Process

In his book, *How We Think*, Dewey speculated about how individuals think when they engage in "conscious inquiry" designed to overcome "perplexity, confusion, or doubt" and to reach some basis for their beliefs. He referred to that type of deliberate thought process as reflective thinking.[59] When McBurney and Hance associated discussion with inquiry, they began to see a relationship, first noted by Dashiell,[60] between the "conscious inquiry" of individuals as described by Dewey, and the

---

[54]McBurney and Hance, *Discussion in Human Affairs*, p. 153.
[55]Crowell, *Discussion: Method of Democracy*, pp. 56–59.
[56]Wagner and Arnold, *Handbook of Group Discussion*, pp. 40–43.
[57]Harnack and Fest, *Group Discussion: Theory and Technique*, pp. 48–71.
[58]Barnlund and Haiman, *The Dynamics of Discussion*, pp. 53–70.
[59]Dewey, *How We Think*.
[60]J. F. Dashiell, "Experimental Studies of the Influence of Social Situations on the Behavior of Individual Human Adults," in *Handbook of Social Psychology*, ed. Carl Murchison (Worcester, Mass.: Clark U. Press, 1935), p. 1131.

conscious or deliberate efforts engaged in by discussion group members when they attempt to solve problems. Consequently, McBurney and Hance proceeded to develop and prescribe a constructive problem-solving procedure for groups to follow that was based upon the Dewey analysis.[61] Various adaptations for discussion groups of Dewey's reflective thinking process have subsequently appeared in most discussion texts. The adaptations have generally involved some or all of the following steps.

Step One: Problem Identification.

To solve a problem effectively, group members should agree on what the problem is and have a good understanding of it. Hence, the first obligation of a discussion group is to carefully define and delimit the problem it is attempting to solve.

Step Two: Problem Analysis.

After the nature of the problem is understood, it is important to analyze or to diagnose the difficulty by examining the problem as thoroughly as possible. Step two is essentially a data-gathering phase, for it involves the collecting and sharing of information about the causes of the problem, its history, the factors that are influencing the problem, the manifestations of the problem, etc.

Step Three: Criteria for Evaluating Solutions.

The criteria step is the most controversial and some textbook writers omit it. It involves the explicit identification of standards that will be used by the group to judge the various solutions to the problem that are generated in step four. The controversy related to this step grows out of the belief by some that a group's success is not related to the existence of criteria for evaluating solutions. Be that as it may, the third step, when employed, involves the explicit agreement on standards that are often formulated by finishing the statement: "Any solution to the problem should. . . ." Criteria might consist of such assertions as: "Any solution to the problem should be economical, . . . should be acceptable to every group member, . . . should be workable, . . . should not generate ill will among nongroup members," etc.

Step Four: Possible Solutions and Their Consequences.

The fourth step in the reflective thinking process consists of the identification of possible solutions to the problem and the possible

[61]McBurney and Hance, *Discussion in Human Affairs*, pp. 65–84.

advantages and disadvantages of each. Groups are encouraged to generate as many solutions as possible and then to narrow them down to four or five choice solutions by carefully considering the consequences of adopting each one.

Step Five: Selection and Testing of Best Solution.

The final step in the reflective thinking process is to agree on the best solution to the problem and, if possible, to test that solution. Theoreticaly, the group could test other solutions if the one initially selected as best proved to be less attractive after the evidence was in.

Alternatives to the Reflective Thinking Process

TRUNCATED PROBLEMS

Barnlund and Haiman point out that groups often deal with "truncated" problems, that is, with problems that can be solved without going through all of the steps in the reflective thinking process.[62] Such problems require a modified or restricted use of the reflective steps. Groups, for example, occasionally are given a problem that has been identified and analyzed, and they are asked merely to recommend a list of possible solutions that will then be considered by another group or authority figure. Such groups need only to focus on step four and to come up with possible solutions to the problem. Other groups may be given a number of possible solutions to a problem and may be asked merely to judge each solution and to come up with the best one. Such groups might restrict themselves to the identification of criteria for evaluating solutions (step three), and to step five, the selection and testing of a solution or solutions.

BRAINSTORMING

Harnack and Fest, Brilhart, and Barnlund and Haiman[63] are some of the discussion textbook writers who have been influenced by the contributions of Osborn[64] and others in the area of brainstorming. Brainstorming is a procedure for encouraging creativity in discussion groups by eliminating or reducing those factors that inhibit the formulation

---

[62]Barnlund and Haiman, *The Dynamics of Discussion*, pp. 91–93.

[63]Harnack and Fest, *Group Discussion: Theory and Technique*, pp. 83–84; Brilhart, *Effective Group Discussion*, pp. 34–35; Barnlund and Haiman, *The Dynamics of Discussion*, pp. 91–93.

[64]Alex F. Osborn, *Applied Imagination: Principles and Procedures of Creative Thinking* (New York: Scribner's, 1953).

and expression of new and creative ideas. Brainstorming could be used by a group to develop criteria for judging solutions, to generate possible solutions to a problem, or even to develop new procedures for testing possible solutions to a problem. To brainstorm, group members must agree to adhere to some of the following rules:

1. Ideas or problem solutions are to be expressed freely, without waiting for one's turn or asking for permission to speak.
2. No one is allowed to criticize anything expressed. Both positive and negative criticism are to be avoided.
3. Wild, offbeat ideas are encouraged.
4. As many ideas as possible should be generated. Quantity will eventually result in quality.

Brainstorming is not viewed as a complete problem-solving procedure by most discussion texts. However, it is seen as a technique that can enhance a discussion group's problem-solving effectiveness.

Other alternatives to the reflective thinking process such as PERT, an industrial problem-solving strategy adopted for discussion purposes by Brilhart and Jochem, [65] Bayless, [66] Philips, [67] and others, are included in some discussion texts. Not all discussion texts insist that a group should solve problems in a systematic and deliberate way. Barnlund and Haiman, for example, point out that there are disadvantages and advantages associated with either adopting a specific problem-solving procedure or simply "diving into" a problem in a free and spontaneous manner.[68] Some of the major strategies for systematically examining a problem in a group have now been considered, and at this point we will examine specific member skills associated with effective discussion by many discussion texts.

Member Skills

Discussion texts have traditionally associated certain member skills or abilities with effective discussion. The general assumption was that if members of discussion groups could become more proficient in these skills, the quality of their performance as discussion group members and

---

[65]J. K. Brilhart and L. M. Jochem, "Effects of Different Patterns on Outcomes of Problem Solving Discussion," *Journal of Applied Psychology* 48 (1964): 175–179.

[66]O. L. Bayless, "An Alternate Pattern for Problem-Solving Discussion," *Journal of Communication* 17, no. 3 (1967): 44–48.

[67]G. M. Phillips, "'PERT' as a Logical Adjunct to the Discussion Process," *Journal of Communication* 15 (1965): 89–99.

[68]Barnlund and Haiman, *The Dynamics of Discussion*, pp. 72–74.

the quality of their group's performance would be enhanced. These skills can be divided into three broad categories: reasoning skills, human relations skills, and communication skills. Some of the elements in each category will be identified and briefly examined in the following sections.

Reasoning Skills

If information presented in a discussion group is to assist the group members to solve a problem, that information must be processed in some way. If the information consists of personal or authoritative opinions, if data of one kind or another are presented, or if arguments are given that are based upon certain assumptions or general principles, those opinions, data, or arguments must be interpreted. Hopefully, the inferences that are drawn will be valid. To assist group participants in the interpretation of information and in the drawing of valid inferences, discussion texts have considered the use of authority, described different types of reasoning, discussed the making of deductive inferences, and identified fallacies or errors in reasoning.

Authority

The opinions of an authority or an expert are often offered as evidence in a discussion. Factual data also may involve authority evidence, Howell and Smith point out, if the identification of the source of the data enhances or diminishes their significance.[69] In our complex world, we must all rely on authority some of the time. No one person or group knows enough or has the facilities to check everything out directly. But a number of tests are provided by discussion texts for evaluating authoritative opinions that are introduced in a discussion. They include the application of such standards as the competency of the authority cited, his or her freedom from bias, whether or not the authority figure could have had possession of the relevant facts, and whether the thinking behind the opinion is stated and appears to be reasonable.

Types of Reasoning

Discussion texts generally distinguish between deductive reasoning and inductive reasoning. Deduction occurs whenever a discussion participant

[69]Howell and Smith, *Discussion*, p. 69.

applies a general principle to a specific case. The use of "formal logic" in discussion is fairly common. It involves the use of such general premises as: "All politicians are liars; Jones is a politician; therefore, Jones is a liar." Crowell[70] and other textbook writers warn that a conclusion that is logically valid may not be true. The syllogism cited above is a case in point. In reality, politician Jones may not be a liar even though the conclusion is logically valid. Crowell differentiates between categorical, disjunctive, and conditional syllogisms.[71] Howell and Smith carefully explain the use of the Venn diagram to identify syllogistic fallacies.[72] Barnlund and Haiman briefly explain deductive reasoning and then state their impression that errors of deduction occur very infrequently in group discussion because they are so easily detected. "Given that all men are mortal," Barnlund and Haiman assert, "it takes no stroke of genius to deduce that Socrates, a man, is therefore mortal."[73] After dismissing fallacies in deductive reasoning as being relatively unimportant to the discussion student, Barnlund and Haiman shift to an examination of inductive reasoning processes, and it is to the inductive realm that we, too, now turn.

Inductive Reasoning

Four principal types of inductive reasoning are examined in most discussion texts. They are reasoning by example, analogy, cause, and sign. Barnlund and Haiman point out that reasoning by analogy is largely a deductive rather than an inductive process,[74] but analogy has usually been classified by discussion texts as an inductive method. Since this chapter is a summary of traditional concerns and outlooks, we are content to classify it that way.

EXAMPLE

Reasoning by example is also called generalization. It involves the making of a generalization about a population of events on the basis of an examination of a sample of those events. Statements about the attitudes of Americans based upon interviews with just a sample of the population involve reasoning by example. Most discussion texts caution discussants to make sure (1) that the generalizations they make or en-

---

70Crowell, *Discussion: Method of Democracy*, p. 108.
71Ibid., pp. 108–14.
72Howell and Smith, *Discussion*, pp. 144–55.
73Barnlund and Haiman, *The Dynamics of Discussion*, p. 142.
74Ibid., pp. 141–42.

counter are based upon enough examples (a sample of adequate size), (2) that the examples are representative of the population being generalized about, (3) that the generalization which may have been true at one time is still relevant, and (4) that examples that would lead to alternative conclusions have not been ignored.

ANALOGY

McBurney and Hance point out that an analogy is essentially a comparison of two cases. In one case, a particular event is known to have occurred and in the second, this event is under question. A discussant reasoning by analogy asserts that since the two cases are alike in other important respects, they probably will be alike "in the respect under question."[75] If the two cases are members of the same class or fall in the same category, the analogy is a literal one. When the two cases are not from the same class (changing horses in the middle of a stream and changing presidents in the middle of a war), the analogy is figurative. An analogy used in a discussion may be faulty if the two cases being compared are clearly not comparable in some important respects. But analogies are tricky. An analogy may be accurate despite the existence of major differences between the two cases, and it may be faulty despite our inability to find major differences between the two cases in areas outside the event under question.

CAUSE

Despite a growing awareness that causality is extremely difficult to establish, the social, economic, and political topics examined by discussion groups often involve a determination of cause or causes. Juvenile delinquency, we insist, is "caused" by broken homes or urban slums. Smoking, we claim, is the cause of lung cancer, and automobiles cause pollution. In discussion groups, we reason from effect to cause and from cause to effect. Claimed causal relationships can be challenged by carefully examining the information upon which they are based. Alternative explanations may be just as plausible. The fact that two events occur in sequence with great regularity does not mean that one is the cause of the other. Correlation is not causation. Gulley points out that the discussant must determine if the proposed cause is a "sufficient explanation" for the effect.[76] Oversimplification is a great danger when dealing with complex phenomena.

[75]McBurney and Hance, *Discussion in Human Affairs*, p. 101.
[76]Gulley, *Discussion, Conference, and Group Process*, p. 147.

SIGN

Reasoning by sign is difficult, dangerous, and yet quite useful in discussion when you deal with a topic where causal relations are very hard to establish. The medical doctor reasons by sign when he uses such signs as fever and a runny nose to infer that his patient has the flu. Sign relationships do not imply that one event is the cause of the other; they merely signal that when one thing is present, so is another. For example, an increase in the number of bankruptcies filed may be a sign of a declining economy, but not necessarily the cause of the decline. The appearance of a number of robins may be a sign of spring, but certainly not the cause of it. Gulley suggests two questions that can be asked to test sign arguments: (1) Are enough signs offered to make the inference that is being drawn seem reasonable? (2) Is the inference suggested by signs supported by other forms of reasoning?[77]

Fallacies

Errors in reasoning are often referred to as fallacies. A number of texts identify and discuss common fallacies in order to help discussants avoid and defend themselves against such errors. Discussants are warned to watch out for ad hominem arguments that shift attention away from a line of reasoning to the personality of the speaker, non sequiturs that attempt to establish a spurious causal relationship, the extending of a reasonable argument to the point where it becomes invalid, and many other errors of thinking.

Interpersonal Relations

The early discussion texts placed greater stress on systematic group inquiry and careful reasoning than they did on good interpersonal relations. However, the early textbook writers did not ignore the socioemotional aspects of group interaction. McBurney and Hance, for example, devoted an entire chapter to "Interpersonal Relations in Discussion."[78] Logic and systematic inquiry have remained important over the years, but more recent discussion textbook writers have explored the socioemotional aspects of group interaction with greater care.

[77]Ibid., pp. 152–53.
[78]McBurney and Hance, *Discussion in Human Affairs*, pp. 259–70.

They have also drawn more concepts from the group dynamics and small-group literature than their predecessors did. The following sections will examine some of the interpersonal problems that discussion texts have considered, as well as some of the small-group concepts that have been explored by these texts.

Even the earliest discussion texts recognized that the way group members responded to each other as individuals would influence their task effectiveness. But their approach to interpersonal matters was in a number of instances based largely on good common sense rather than on the scholarly literature dealing with personal and interpersonal behavior. For example, in their chapter devoted to interpersonal relations McBurney and Hance identified (in a delightful, if not profound, way) the roles people play in groups, and they advised discussants to reward constructive behavior, to probe disruptive behavior by asking questions, and always to act as if the motives of others were honorable.[79] Howell and Smith encouraged discussion group members to "come to understand one another," because understanding is likely to lead to improved interpersonal relationships.[80] But it was not until the 1960s that discussion texts began to deal with interpersonal relations in a manner that reflected an understanding of both the research literature dealing with interpersonal phenomena and the group training laboratories and other developments associated with the human relations movement.

More recent discussion textbooks reflect a sophistication in the interpersonal area that earlier texts lacked. Some of these texts examine the implications of the attractions and repulsions that group members feel toward one another as revealed by sociometric tests. Others discuss the implications of various research studies such as the investigation by Deutsch (1949), who found fewer communication problems in cooperative groups than in competitive groups, or the studies by Horowitz, Lyons, and Perlmutter (1951) and by Bach (1951) that found relationships between the tendencies to agree with or to be influenced by a group member and the tendency to like the member,[81] or the investigations in the area of conformity by Asch (1951) and by Schachter (1953) that demonstrated the strength of social pressure in groups, especially in groups that are cohesive.[82] The influence of the human relations movement was reflected in the greater stress placed by some texts on social sensitivity and on interpersonal feedback and group self-evaluation.[83]

[79]Ibid.
[80]Howell and Smith, *Discussion*, p. 177.
[81]Gulley, *Discussion, Conference, and Group Process*, pp. 97–98.
[82]Barnlund and Haiman, *The Dynamics of Discussion*, p. 102.
[83]Gulley, *Discussion, Conference, and Group Process*, p. 98; Barnlund and Haiman, *The Dynamics of Discussion*, p. 238.

In addition to their greater interest in the research literature dealing with interpersonal relations and their awareness of developments in the human relations training area, more recent discussion texts also examine a number of concepts prevalent in the small-group literature that appear to be helpful in understanding the discussion process. These concepts are reviewed in the following section.

Small-Group Concepts

Although such concepts as group size, power relationships in groups, apathy, hostility, and group cohesiveness have received elaborate attention in one discussion text or another, some of the small-group variables that have been given the greatest amount of emphasis in recent discussion texts are roles, group norms, social climate, and conformity or social pressure. All of these latter concepts are discussed elsewhere in this text. They are briefly described here to provide an awareness of how the concepts have been treated in the discussion literature.

ROLE

Most discussion texts have defined role as the functions that a discussant performs in a group. These functions may involve giving opinions, clarifying the remarks of others, or a variety of other task or process behaviors. The most distinctive approach to roles is provided by Bormann, who defines roles on the basis of the expectations of discussion participants. Bormann studied roles as they emerged in leaderless discussion groups and noted two general tendencies: (1) group members reinforce the role behaviors that they perceive to be most helpful to the group, and (2) group members are "channeled" into performing those functions that they can handle most efficiently.[84]

GROUP NORMS

Norms regulate the behavior of group members. They consist of the notions group members have about how they ought to behave. Norms fall into patterns and become predictable aspects of a group's activities and point of view. The members of groups that have a strong "honesty" norm are likely to behave honestly toward each other, and they will be "friendly" toward each other if that, too, is a group norm.

[84]Bormann, *Discussion and Group Methods*, p. 197.

SOCIAL CLIMATE

Atmosphere or social climate refers to the characteristic ways members interact with one another in a group. The social climate may be formal or informal, relaxed or tense, happy or sad, etc. Barnlund and Haiman view social climate as a reflection of a group's norm system. Some groups, they point out, may have a social climate that is overly cooperative, whereas others may be overly competitive. Groups may also have social climates that are anarchic, ritualistic, or interdependent.[85]

CONFORMITY

The tendency of a group to pressure its members to conform to group norms and standards has long been recognized. The member who deviates from a group norm will be encouraged to change his behavior and, in some cases, he will be punished if he fails to get into line. Discussion specialists probably have been intrigued with the concept of conformity because conformity, as well as the pressure to conform, manifests itself in the communication behavior of the group members. Hence, we now turn to an examination of the way discussion texts have explored the communication process in small groups.

Communication and Language Behavior

It has been pointed out that the contemporary group communication scholar is more interested in studying the communication process in small groups than the traditionalist in discussion has been. Traditional discussion texts have not ignored communication phenomena. They have often focused, however, on communication and language behavior in small groups not primarily to better understand the process but to give suggestions about how discussants could improve their speaking.

The elements of good speech noted in most discussion texts are quite similar. They suggest that a discussant's speech should be animated, sincere, easy to understand, direct, unobtrusive, and natural. The discussant should also use appropriate body action, exhibit poise, and be a good listener. A number of texts make specific suggestions about language and the importance of using it accurately. Gulley discusses referents and different levels of abstraction,[86] Cartright and Hinds stress

[85]Barnlund and Haiman, *The Dynamics of Discussion*, pp. 193–97.
[86]Gulley, *Discussion, Conference, and Group Process*, pp. 168–70.

the importance of indexing,[87] and Barnlund and Haiman examine language and thought relationships and the problems associated with polarity (talking in terms of opposites) and abstracting (the failure to recognize the different levels at which people talk).[88]

Many texts consider various ways to examine message behavior in groups, but they approach the subject in an indirect manner. Gulley, for example, discusses various category systems for analyzing group interaction in a chapter devoted to group evaluation,[89] and Bormann discusses content analysis in a section of his text devoted to social climates.[90] Communication networks are examined by Barnlund and Haiman in a chapter devoted to obstacles to communication.[91] Message analysis need not be approached directly to be understood or appreciated. Nevertheless, it is worthwhile to note that these analytical methods have been primarily used in discussion texts to achieve a prescriptive goal, not merely to acquaint the reader with a strategy for examining group interaction. Harnack and Fest's use of communication theory to analyze the source-encoder, message, channel, and decoder-receiver in discussion groups represents a significant step forward in the movement of communication scholars toward the development of group communication as an area of study and research.[92]

Conclusion

This chapter explains the historical base upon which the present text is built. The summary of the discussion textbook literature was not meant to be complete or exhaustive. Not all discussion textbooks were covered and those that were examined were not analyzed thoroughly. Important topics covered by a number of texts were ignored completely. Nevertheless, we believe that the overview was sufficient to demonstrate that, for the most part, discussion texts in the past have been more concerned with prescription than with description. They have paid more attention to the task aspects of discussion than to the socioemotional aspects, but the balance has shifted somewhat over the years. Recent discussion texts incude more social psychological data about small groups and reflect a greater awareness of group dynamics orientations associated with group training and development. Except perhaps for certain portions of Barnlund and Haiman, Harnack and

[87]Cartright and Hinds, *Creative Discussion*, pp. 118–20.

[88]Barnlund and Haiman, *The Dynamics of Discussion*, pp. 262–65.

[89]Gulley, *Discussion, Conference and Group Process*, pp. 347–55.

[90]Bormann, *Discussion and Group Methods*, pp. 162–63.

[91]Barnlund and Haiman, *The Dynamics of Discussion*, pp. 247–54.

[92]Harnack and Fest, *Group Discussion: Theory and Technique*, pp. 406–19.

Fest, and Bormann, however, none of the texts examined are devoted· primarily to the explication of group communication as an area of study, research, and application. The next chapter, devoted to communication observation systems, is designed to move us closer to that goal.

SUMMARY

1. Group discussion first established itself as a vital part of the speech communication curriculum in the late 1930s. The area was then referred to as discussion.

2. Discussion texts have traditionally dealt more with prescription than with description, and more with task aspects of discussion than with socioemotional aspects. None of them have dealt primarily with the explication of group communication as an area of study, research, and application.

3. Discussion has been viewed traditionally as a problem-solving activity involving two or more people communicating orally face-to-face and under the direction of a leader.

4. Discussion is a particularly relevant area of study in the United States because democracy cannot function without discussion.

5. The growth of discussion since the turn of the century can be attributed to a number of factors: urbanization (which necessitated greater interdependence), advances in scientific method and the desire of scholars to apply it to human affairs, the increasing pragmatism of higher education, "concurrent developments," and deliberate attempts to promote the use of discussion.

6. Two types of reasoning are distinguished in the discussion literature: deductive and inductive. Of the two, inductive reasoning is the more troublesome and therefore the more important to the discussion student.

7. Early discussion texts placed more stress on systematic group inquiry and careful reasoning than they did on good interpersonal relations. However, they did not ignore socioemotional factors.

8. Concepts useful in understanding the discussion process include: roles, group norms, social climate, and conformity.

9. Traditionally, discussion texts have focused on communication and language behavior in small groups in order to give suggestions about how discussants could improve their speaking rather than to better understand the process of group communication.

10. Message analysis methods were primarily used in discussion texts to achieve a prescriptive goal, rather than to acquaint the reader with a strategy for examining group interaction.

toward
effective
group
communication

observing
group communication

━━━━━━━━━━━━━━━━━━━━━━━━━━━━━━ 5

OBJECTIVES

After studying this chapter, you should be able to:

Describe five observation systems.

Recognize observation systems as methods for better understanding the complicated phenomenon of group communication.

Begin to use these systems to organize your own observations of group communication phenomena.

Realize the utility of comparing your observations with those of other group members.

In one sense, every concept we have introduced to this point and every concept we will introduce hereafter contribute to a set of perspectives from which group communication phenomena may be viewed. But whereas any introductory book on almost any subject provides you with perspectives from which to view particular phenomena, a book on group communication deals with such a potentially complex and confusing phenomenon that we must approach it with somewhat more structure than we would employ in approaching other phenomena. The very complexity of group processes has stimulated social scientists from a variety of academic points of view to develop an amazing array of observation and recording systems designed to identify and categorize certain events occurring in groups or certain properties of groups. These observation and recording systems have three general purposes: (1) By providing a basis on which to isolate and differentiate group phenomena, they assist those who would construct theories of group process. 2) By allowing "judges" or "observers" to express their observations in quantified terms, they allow for the generation of "data" useful in research which tests and refines theories of group process. (3) By providing categories into which events may be classified or by providing continua along which group and individual properties may be rated, they provide implicit strategies for making sense out of group processes.

We assume that your interests are not yet those of constructing theories or doing formal research on group communication. We assume that your interests, presently, are in making sense of your own experiences in groups. Consequently, even though most of the observation systems we will describe in this chapter were developed originally for use as research tools, we will present them simply as ways of structuring your observations of group communication phenomena.

Some preliminary comments on observation systems in general may help you better understand the specific observation systems described in this chapter. First, observation systems may vary in the extent to which refined judgments are required of an observer. A relatively simple judgment may be called for if you are counting "the number of times" each group member "talks" during a thirty-minute discussion period. A somewhat more complicated judgment is called for if you were to add to the preceding example the observation of "who talks to whom." An even more complicated judgment is called for if you were to decide whether a given communicative act should be characterized as "managerial-autocratic," or "docile-dependent." All the observation systems we will describe in this chapter require relatively complicated judgments. Hence, the observations growing out of these systems may reasonably be called "subjective." That your observations of group communication will be subjective is understandable. To the extent that your observations agree with those of others who have viewed the same events, however, your observations may be called "intersubjective." Intersubjectivity (an old philosophy of science term which has been replaced by the contemporary term "reliability") implies that our confidence in our judgment should increase to the extent that other individuals describe the same events in the same ways that we have described these events. So, even though observation systems are typically "subjective," we assume that you will take advantage of any opportunities you might have for comparing your observations with those of others.

Categories and Ratings

A second comment about observation systems is that they are distinguishable into two general types. There are category systems and rating

system. *A category system* is one in which events are individually classified according to preestablished categories. For example, in a recent
investigation of problem solving and informal group discussions, researchers classified each individual member statement into one of the
following categories:[1]

1. Initiates and develops a theme
2. Agrees with expressed position
3. Disagrees with expressed position
4. Gives information
5. Asks for information

Given a set of categories, you, as an observer, must decide what
basic events or units will be classified according to these categories.
Your "units of observation," that is, those phenomena which are to be
classified according to the preestablished categories, are defined to suit
your own observation purposes. Characteristically, units are defined at
one of three levels: (1) utterances; (2) themes; (3) participants. *Utterances*
are individual member statements, sometimes defined as sentences, sometimes as completed thoughts, and sometimes as the continuous and uninterrupted flow of language emitted by a specific group member. (That
is, person A's "utterance" is completed when he stops and person B
begins talking.) *Themes* are continuous lines of thought sharing a common or central content. Themes may include utterances by more than
one group member. For example, "promoting harmony" might be one
of several categories employed in a thematic analysis of group communication. The theme would be interpreted as having occurred once so
long as one or more utterances were, at some point in the group's
interaction, directed toward "promoting harmony." Finally, the observation unit might be defined so broadly as to categorize participants in
terms of the category which best characterizes the behavior of each
individual group member. Again, the definition of the unit to be observed
and classified is a function of your purposes in making observations.

A second basic strategy in making observations employs the use of
rating scales. Instead of classifying units into preestablished categories,
however, units are rated along one or more continua. A continuum
implies varying degrees to which a particular characteristic is present.
For example, individual group members (the observational units) may
be rated by you (the observer) in terms of the extent to which a given
member "influenced the ultimate group decision" the characteristic
which presumably varies from member to member or unit to unit) along

---

[1]Dennis S. Gouran and John E. Baird, Jr., "An Analysis of Distributional and
Sequential Structure in Problem-Solving and Informal Group Discussion," *Speech
Monographs* 39 (1972): 16–22.

a continuum ranging from "a great deal" (scale interval number one) to "not at all" (scale interval number seven). The observation systems to be described later in this chapter will provide further explanation and illustration of both category systems and rating scales.

Intellective and Interpersonal Systems

A final distinction that should be made concerns the extent to which observation systems focus upon group commcnication behavior that is directed toward solving problems, making decisions, or formulating judgments (intellective systems), and those observation systems that focus upon communication behavior involved in the development and maintenance of interpersonal sentiments (interpersonal systems). Intellective processes involve ways in which groups deliberate, and member communicative behaviors which bear upon those deliberations. Interpersonal processes involve ways in which member feelings and sentiments are conveyed, or member communicative behaviors which serve as the basis for the development and maintenance of sentiment relationships in groups. This distinction is not absolute. Almost all collective reasoning processes are influenced by, and allow for, the manifestation of interpersonal sentiments. "Providing support" and "encouraging" are forms of behavior that might be included in either an intellective or an interpersonal system. If the support or encouragement were directed toward another member's ideas, proposals, or suggestions, the system would probably be intellective. If the support or encouragement were directed primarily toward another group member as an individual, the system would probably be interpersonal. The distinction is not absolute, but is one of relative emphasis. Intellective systems emphasize member communicative behavior directed primarily toward the completion of a task, the solving of a problem, or the formulation of a collective judgment. Interpersonal systems emphasize member communicative behavior directed primarily toward the development, maintenance, or expression of sentiment relationships between members of the group, or between members and the group as a whole.

Some Illustrative Observation Systems

We will describe five illustrative observation systems. These systems have been chosen because of their potential usefulness to you in observing group communication phenomena. Although all of the systems to be described in this chapter were developed originally for theory building and/or research uses, we have included them because of their utility as observation guides for ongoing group communication processes. Each of the five systems concerns itself with individual member communication behavior. Other systems are available and may be consulted if you have specific observational purposes not met by the five systems we have selected.[2]

I. FUNCTIONAL ROLES

An early observation system, one still frequently used in educational settings, is that developed by Benne and Sheats.[3] At the First National Training Laboratory in Group Development, in 1947, Benne and Sheats analyzed the participation of group members in terms of the functional roles performed by group members during group deliberations. A general empirical purpose of the analysis was to shift the attention of researchers away from what had been traditionally a focus upon the traits and qualities assumed to be inherent in formal or designated "leaders." Benne and Sheats considered it equally important, if not more important, to observe and code member roles, specifically as these roles might function instrumentally in accomplishing group purposes. As we shall see in Chapter 6's discussion of leadership, the functional approach to the study of leadership, which includes the leadership behaviors of group members as well as formal leaders, did supplant the traits approach to the study of leadership and continues to be a dominant strategy in understanding leadership.

This observation system is an intellective one. The observation of member participation resulted in lists of member-roles, arranged into three broad categories. (1) Group task roles are related to the task on which the group is working. The forms of behavior described under *group task roles* are clearly behaviors that relate to the group's formulation and expression of collective judgment. (2) Group building and maintenance roles relate to the manner in which the group performs its task. The forms of behavior described under *group building and maintenance roles* are clearly behaviors that influence the group's way of working, and that build and maintain a group-centered attitude on the part of group members. (3) Individual roles relate to the satisfaction of individual needs. The forms of behavior described under *individual roles* clearly describe behavior that is not necessarily directed toward accomplishment of a task, or the development and maintenance of working

[2]As a starting reference, see Edgar F. Borgatta and Betty Crowther, *A Workbook for the Study of Social Interaction Process* (Chicago: Rand McNally, 1965).

[3]Kenneth D. Benne and Paul Sheats, "Functional Roles of Group Members," *Journal of Social Issues* 4 (Spring 1948): 41–49.

relationships that might facilitate the accomplishment of a task. Individual roles are assumed to be directed toward the satisfaction of individual needs, as seen by the individual performing the role.

Familiarity with the roles is useful in observing ways in which group members facilitate or impede group task performance in their direct contributions to formulation of collective judgment (task roles), in their building and maintenance of working relationships (group building and maintenance roles), or in their pursuit of individual needs (individual roles). It is important to remember that a given group member may perform a variety of roles, including roles in each of the three broad categories. Nevertheless, it is interesting to observe the extent to which particular group members characteristically perform certain roles. In reading through the following list with its descriptions of behavior, you may call to mind from your recent experiences group members who may be characterized as performing predominantly one or several roles.

Group Task Roles

The following analysis assumes that the task of the discussion group is to select, define and solve common problems. The roles are identified in relation to functions of facilitation and coordination of group problem-solving activities. Each member may of course enact more than one role in any given unit of participation and a wide range of roles in successive participations. Any or all of these roles may be played at times by the group "leader" as well as by various members.

a. The *initiator-contributor* suggests or proposes to the group new ideas or a changed way of regarding the group problem or goal. The novelty proposed may take the form of suggestions of a new group goal or a new definition of the problem. It may take the form of a suggested solution or some way of handling a difficulty that the group has encountered. Or it may take the form of a proposed new procedure for the group, a new way of organizing the group for the task ahead.

b. The *information seeker* asks for clarification of suggestions made in terms of their factual adequacy, for authoritative information and facts pertinent to the problem being discussed.

c. The *opinion seeker* asks not primarily for the facts of the case but for a clarification of the values pertinent to what the group is undertaking or of values involved in a suggestion made or in alternative suggestions.

d. The *information giver* offers facts or generalizations which are "authoritative" or relates his own experience pertinently to the group problem.

e. The *opinion giver* states his belief or opinion pertinently to a suggestion made or to alternate suggestions. The emphasis is on his proposal of what should become the group's view of pertinent values, not primarily upon relevant facts or information.

f. The *elaborator* spells out suggestions in terms of examples or developed meanings, offers a rationale for suggestions previously made and tries to deduce how an idea or suggestion would work out if adopted by the group.

g. The *coordinator* shows or clarifies the relationships among various ideas and suggestions, tries to pull ideas and suggestions together or tries to coordinate the activities of various members or sub-groups.

h. The *orienter* defines the position of the group with respect to its goals by summarizing what has occurred, points to departures from agreed upon directions or goals, or raises questions about the direction which the group discussion is taking.

i. The *evaluator-critic* subjects the accomplishment of the group to some standard or set of standards of group-functioning in the context of the group task. Thus, he may evaluate or question the "practicality," the "logic," the "facts," or the "procedure" of a suggestion or of some unit of group discussion.

j. The *energizer* prods the group to action or decision, attempts to stimulate or arouse the group to "greater" or "higher quality" activity.

k. The *procedural technician* expedites group movement by doing things for the group—performing routine tasks, e.g., distributing materials, or manipulating objects for the group, e.g., rearranging the seating or running the recording machine, etc.

l. The *recorder* writes down suggestions, makes a record of group decisions, or writes down the product of discussion. The recorder role is the "group memory."

Group Building and Maintenance Roles

Here the analysis of member-functions is oriented to those participations which have for their purpose the building of group-centered attitudes and orientation among the members of a group or the maintenance and perpetuation of such group-centered behavior. A given contribution may involve several roles and a member or the "leader" may perform various roles in successive contributions.

a. The *encourager* praises, agrees with and accepts the contribution of others. He indicates warmth and solidarity in his attitude toward other group members, offers commendation and praise and in various ways indicates understanding and acceptance of other points of view, ideas and suggestions.

b. The *harmonizer* mediates the differences between other members, attempts to reconcile disagreements, relieves tension in conflict situations through jesting or pouring oil on the troubled waters, etc.

c. The *compromiser* operates from within a conflict in which his idea or position is involved. He may offer compromise by yielding status, admitting his error, by disciplining himself to maintain group harmony, or by "coming half-way" in moving along with the group.

d. The *gate-keeper and expediter* attempts to keep communication channels open by encouraging or facilitating the participation of others ("We haven't got the ideas of Mr. X yet," etc.) or by proposing regulation of the flow of communication ("Why don't we limit the length of our contributions so that everyone will have chance to contribute?" etc.).

e. The *standard-setter* or *ego ideal* expresses standards for the group to attempt to achieve in its functioning or applies standards in evaluating the quality of group processes.

f. The *group-observer and commentator* keeps records of various aspects of group process and feeds such data with proposed interpretations into the group's evaluation of its own procedures.

g. The *follower* goes along with the movement of the group, more or less passively accepting the ideas of others, serving as an audience in group discussion and decision.

"Individual" Roles

Attempts by "members" of a group to satisfy individual needs which are irrelevant to the group task and which are non-oriented or negatively oriented to group building and maintenance set problems of group and member training. A high incident of "individual-centered" as opposed to "group centered" participation in a group always calls for self-diagnosis of the group. The diagnosis may reveal one or several of a number of conditions—low level of skill-training among members, including the group leader; the prevalence of "authoritarian" and "laissez faire" points of view toward group functioning in the group; a low level of group maturity, discipline and morale; an inappropriately chosen and inadequately defined group task, etc. Whatever the diagnosis, it is in this setting that the training needs of the group are to be discovered and group training efforts to meet these needs are to be defined. The outright "suppression" of "individual roles" will deprive the group of data needed for really adequate self-diagnosis and therapy.

a. The *aggressor* may work in many ways—deflating the status of others, expressing disapproval of the values, acts or feelings of others, attacking the group or the problem it is working on, joking aggressively, showing envy toward another's contribution by trying to take credit for it, etc.

b. The *blocker* tends to be negativistic and stubbornly resistant, disagreeing and opposing without or beyond "reason" and attempting to maintain or bring back an issue after the group had rejected or bypassed it.

c. The *recognition-seeker* works in various ways to call attention to himself, whether through boasting, reporting on personal achievements, acting in unusual ways, struggling to prevent his being placed in an "inferior" position, etc.

d. The *self-confessor* uses the audience opportunity which the group setting provides to express personal, non-group oriented, "feeling," "insight," "ideology," etc.

e. The *playboy* makes a display of his lack of involvement in the group's processes. This may take the form of cynicism, nonchalance, horseplay and other more or less studied forms of "out of field" behavior.

f. The *dominator* tries to assert authority or superiority in manipulating the group or certain members of the group. This domination may take the form of flattery, of asserting a superior status or right to attention, giving directions authoritatively, interrupting the contributions of others, etc.

g. The *help-seeker* attempts to call forth "sympathy" response from other group members or from the whole group, whether through expressions of insecurity, personal confusion or depreciation of himself beyond "reason."

h. The *special interest pleader* speaks for the "small business man," the "grass roots" community, the "housewife," "labor," etc., usually cloaking his own prejudices or biases in the stereotype which best fits his individual need.[4]

II. BALES'S INTERACTION PROCESS ANALYSIS

One of the most widely used category systems is that developed by Bales.[5] An early category system, it was developed primarily as a research tool and is probably the most widely used guide for the structured, empirical observation of group member behavior. It has utility also in the conduct of classroom observations and informal group observations not directed toward a highly structured empirical purpose. Although Bales's category system has undergone several revisions, we will present and discuss an early version which we have found to be more readily understood and more easily used than are later versions.[6] Some general comments might help to introduce this category system.

First, the observer employing this category system is assumed to have access to the culture base of the group, so that a frame of reference common to the group may be adopted in order for the observer properly to interpret the meaning of the interaction units he is observing.

Second, the observer is asked to make his observations as if he were a member of the group in question. It is suggested that the observer keep in mind the general question: "If this fellow (the actor) were acting toward me (the group member) in this way, what would his act mean to me?"[7]

Third, the unit of interaction to be scored is "the smallest discriminable segment of verbal or nonverbal behavior to which the observer, using the present set of categories after appropriate training, can assign a classification under conditions of continuous serial scoring. This unit may be called an act, or more properly, a single interaction, since all acts in the present scheme are regarded as interactions. The unit as defined here has also been called the single item of thought or the single item of behavior."[8] The unit of interaction to be scored may be a sentence, a clause, a single word, or an entire utterance.

If you were conducting a formal research study, you would need to be trained in the use of this category system. However, we have found

[4]Ibid. Quoted by permission from Kenneth D. Benne and the *Journal of Social Issues.*

[5]Robert F. Bales, *Interaction Process Analysis: A Method for the Study of Small Groups* (Cambridge: Addison-Wesley, 1950).

[6]See Robert F. Bales, *Personality and Interpersonal Behavior* (New York: Holt, Rinehart & Winston, 1970), Appendix 4.

[7]Bales, *Interaction Process Analysis*, p. 41.

[8]Ibid. p. 37.

that the category system is usable in informal observations of classroom interactions without substantial prior training. With this particular category system, we would stress the utility of comparing your observations with those of other group members. The essential features of the category system are represented in Figure 5–1.

The core of the category system consists of the twelve categories

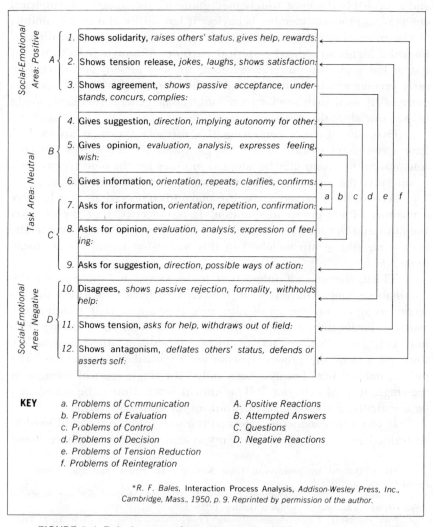

FIGURE 5–1 Bales's categories and general groupings.

Source: From Robert F. Bales, *Interaction Process Analysis: A Method for the Study of Small Groups* (Reading, Mass.: Addison-Wesley, 1950), p. 59. Reprinted by permission of the author.

listed in the center of Figure 5–1. These categories have been system-atically grouped according to the four major forms of behavior identified in the left-hand section of Figure 5–1. There are two major forms of social-emotional behavior, positive and negative reactions, and two major forms of task behavior, attempted answers and questions. Each of these four major forms of behavior has three specific categories associated with it. The middle categories (4 through 9) are concerned primarily with problem-solving tasks and are considered emotionally neutral. The extreme categories are concerned primarily with problems of group organization and integration and are considered emotionally loaded.

The twelve categories are organized somewhat differently in the right-hand section of Figure 5–1. An interacting group is assumed to encounter and to attempt to resolve problems in six general areas: (a) problems involved in arriving at a common definition and mutual under-standing of the situation (orientation); (b) problems involved in identify-ing or developing a shared set of criteria or values by means of which alternative solutions are evaluated (evaluation); (c) problems involved in members influencing each other (control); (d) problems involved in arriving at a collective judgment or decision (decision); (e) problems involved in dealing with the tensions generated during the group's deliberation (tension management); (f) problems involved in maintaining an integrated group (integration).[9]

For simple class-related activities, you can develop a form sheet to record your observations. List the twelve basic categories down the left-hand margin of a sheet. Draw vertical lines down the sheet so that a series of columns is present. Number the columns consecutively at the top of the sheet. When completed, the sheet will consist of a large matrix, the rows defined by the twelve categories and the columns numbered across the top. Each column may be used to record a single interaction unit. When the scoring is completed, the sequence of the interaction units will be recorded and numbered in keeping with the columns. Usually, members are identified by code numbers, from one to N. Who speaks to whom can be recorded simply by a series of coupled numbers. Remarks addressed by members to the group as a whole are indicated by a zero. Thus, 2–0 would refer to group member number 2 addressing the group as a whole.

Whether a group progresses through certain phases in problem solving, whether task and social-emotional behaviors are balanced or disproportionate, whether certain members disproportionately engage in

[9]For an example of how these categories are employed in the formal investiga-tion of group deliberations, see Robert F. Bales and Fred L. Strodtbeck, "Phases in Group Problem Solving," in *Group Dynamics*, 2d ed., ed. Dorwin Cartwright and Alvin Zander (Evanston, Illinois: Row, Peterson, 1960).

specific forms of behavior, whether specific member's behavior vary with respect to the problem phase (orientation, evaluation, control, etc.) through which the group is progressing, whether certain members talk disproportionately to certain other members, whether group interaction assumes a particular form or pattern following decision proposals, and many other questions may be explored tentatively on the basis of your analysis and observation of member behaviors conforming to these twelve basic categories.

III. AN EARLY INTERPERSONAL SYSTEM

The utility of the category system, as far as you are concerned, may not be in the scores it ultimately yields for you to analyze quantitatively. The usefulness of the category system may be in the perspective it provides for viewing and interpreting group communication behavior. The category system at hand is one which we have included primarily for its conceptual perspective. We make no attempt to carry its description to the point where scores are derived or recorded. It is an early interpersonal category system associated principally with the work of Timothy Leary (before Leary became popularly known as "the high priest of drugs").[10]

The conceptual orientation of this category system grows out of an analysis of interpersonal motives. Interpersonal behaviors are assumed to be purposive in nature. The purpose of a given interpersonal behavior is reflected in the kind of relationship the individual is attempting to establish with another by engaging in that interpersonal behavior. A group member may say, "Well, I'm not surprised that no one likes my ideas. That's perfectly all right. It doesn't bother me. No one ever likes my ideas. I haven't understood this discussion very well, and I've had a lot of trouble expressing myself. I guess I'm not as smart as the rest of you." The purpose for engaging in such behavior may be to provoke a response of concern, reassurance, and support from others. Leary's category system is employed to code interpersonal behavior in terms of the motives inferred from those behaviors.

A basic assumption of this conceptual framework is that in many or most instances interpersonal motives are expressed in a reflex manner.

---

[10]M. B. Freedman, T. F. Leary, A. G. Ossorio, and H. S. Coffey, "The Interpersonal Dimension of Personality," *Journal of Personality* 20 (1951): 143–61; T. F. Leary and H. S. Coffey, "Interpersonal Diagnosis: Some Problems of Methodology and Validation," *Journal of Abnormal and Social Psychology* 50 (1955): 110–16; T. F. Leary, "The Theory and Measurement Methodology of Interpersonal Communication," *Psychiatry* 18 (May 1955): 147–61; T. F. Leary, *Interpersonal Diagnosis of Personality: A Functional Theory and Methodology for Personality Evaluation* (New York: Ronald Press, 1957).

Interpersonal behaviors are exhibited so automatically, and responses to others' behaviors occur so spontaneously, and often unwittingly, that social interaction may be seen as a series of interpersonal reflexes. If I cry, you comfort me. If I attack, you are hostile. If I submit, you direct me. The basic notion of the interpersonal reflex is that whereas the initiator behaves purposively in order to evoke certain responses from the other, the other's responses are almost automatic and, in a sense, conditioned. Although we are not always right, we have nevertheless developed a certain sophistication in eliciting responses we wish from others.

Individuals differ in the extent to which they are capable of exhibiting, or characteristically do exhibit, a variety of interpersonal behaviors. Some individuals are motivated by a relatively narrow set of interpersonal goals. Across a wide variety of circumstances and social contexts some individuals exhibit a relatively narrow range of behaviors. The person who is always modest, or always arrogant, or always suspicious, or always trustful, and whose behavior seems unaffected by changes in circumstances, is the person who is assumed to have maladaptive and dysfunctional interpersonal behaviors. The effectively and successfully functioning individual is assumed to possess a wider range of interpersonal behaviors and is characterized by flexibility in exhibiting these behaviors under varying circumstances, social contexts, and with different others.

The basic categories of interpersonal behavior are represented in Figure 5–2. There are sixteen basic mechanisms or reflexes. In Figure 5–2, each of the sixteen mechanisms are illustrated by sample behavior. The inner circle describes what are presumed to be "adaptive" reflexes. To manage, to guide, to ask for help, and to sympathize are acts that most of us engage in at some time. The next outermost ring describes the form of behavior this interpersonal reflex tends to elicit from the other. Thus, those who act aggressively, with firm actions, tend to elicit passive resistance. Those who respect, admire, and conform to others tend to provoke advice. The next outermost circle describes extreme or rigid reflexes. The outermost ring is divided into eight general categories, with each category labeling an adaptive (e.g., "competitive") and an extreme or pathological (e.g., "exploitive") intensity for that category of behavior.

The conceptual framework provided by this category system seems descriptive of many forms of social interaction. With respect to the communicative behaviors of group members, the perspective provided uniquely focuses on the interpersonal mechanisms through which relationships are formed and maintained. In Chapter 3, we referred to the spontaneous and frequently unpredictable manner in which group com-

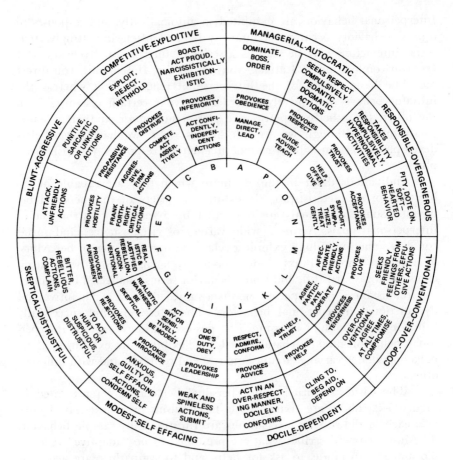

FIGURE 5–2 The basic interpersonal reflexes.

Source: From T. F. Leary, "The Theory and Measurement Methodology of Interpersonal Communication," *Psychiatry*, 18 (May 1955): 147–61. Reprinted by permission.

munication occurs. In group communication, there are undoubtedly processes which underly the explicit content of group communication. These processes are often conditioned by individual motives. Thus, in observing group communication, it is wise to carry to the observation a perspective through which interpersonal mechanisms may be observed, as well as the explicit surface content of group communication.

IV. SIEBURG'S ANALYSIS OF CONFIRMATION

In an intriguing investigation of the communication characteristics of effective and ineffective groups, Sieburg explored a dimension that may prove to be one of the best observational indicators for distinguishing functional and dysfunctional group communication.[11] Deriving her central concepts from existential writings, Sieburg has developed a method for observing group communication in terms of whether member communicative acts are "confirming" or "disconfirming" in nature.[12] The analysis of confirmation and disconfirmation rests upon the identification of ways in which an individual responds to communicative acts of others. Hence, whether a behavior is considered confirming or disconfirming is a function of its relationship to the communicative act that directly preceded it.

Confirming responses are those that presumably cause a person to value himself as an individual. Confirmation implies recognition of, attention to, and in some cases a willingness to affiliate with the other. Disconfirming responses imply that the other person's communicative attempts do not warrant direct acknowledgment or serious attention. Disconfirmation implies a denial of the inherent value of another individual, a failure to attend to, and in some cases an unwillingness to affiliate with, the other. Some examples of disconfirming and confirming responses may help to clarify the nature of this particular communication dimension.

Disconfirming Responses

1. *Impervious response.* When one speaker fails to acknowledge, even minimally, the other speaker's communicative attempt, or when one ignores or disregards the other by not giving any ostensible acknowledgment of the other's communication, his response may be called impervious.

2. *Interrupting response.* When one speaker cuts the other speaker short or begins while the other is still speaking, his response may be called interrupting.

3. *Irrelevant response.* When one speaker responds in a way that seems unrelated to what the other has been saying, or when one speaker introduces a new topic without warning or returns to his earlier topic, apparently disregarding the intervening conversation, his response may be called irrelevant.

4. *Tangential response.* When one speaker acknowledges the other person's communication but immediately takes the conversation in another direction, his response may be called tangential. Occasionally, individuals exhibit what may appear to be direct responses to the other, such as "Yes, but . . ." or "Well, you may be right, but . . . ," but then

---

[11] Evelyn Sieburg, "Dysfunctional Communication and Interpersonal Responsiveness in Small Groups" (Ph.D. diss., University of Denver, 1969).

[12] In her most recent work, currently in progress, Sieburg expanded her interest in groups to include a concern for the development of a general theory of interpersonal confirmation. Cf. Evelyn Sieburg, "Toward a Theory of Interpersonal Confirmation" (unpublished ms., University of Denver, 1972).

may proceed to respond with communicative content very different from or unrelated to that which preceded. Such responses may still be called tangential.

5. *Impersonal response.* When a speaker conducts a monologue, when his speech communication behavior appears intellectualized and impersonal, contains few first-person statements and many generalized "you" or "one" statements, and is heavily loaded with euphemisms or clichés, the response may be called impersonal.

6. *Incoherent response.* When the speaker responds with sentences that are incomplete, or with rambling statements difficult to follow, or with sentences containing much retracing or rephrasing, or interjections such as "you know" or "I mean," his response may be called incoherent.

7. *Incongruous response.* When the speaker engages in nonvocal behavior that seems inconsistent with the vocal content, his response may be called incongruous. For example, "Who's angry? I'm not angry!" (said in a tone and volume that strongly suggests anger). Or, "I'm really concerned about you" (said in a tone that suggests lack of interest or disdain).

Confirming Responses

1. *Direct acknowledgment.* One speaker acknowledges the other's communication and reacts to it directly and verbally.

2. *Agreement about content.* One speaker reinforces or supports information or opinions expressed by the other.

3. *Supportive response.* One speaker expresses understanding of the other, reassures him, or tries to make him feel better.

4. *Clarifying response.* One speaker tries to clarify the content of the other's message or attempts to clarify the other's present or past feelings. The usual form of a clarifying response is to elicit more information, to encourage the other to say more, or to repeat in an inquiring way what was understood.

5. *Expression of positive feeling.* One speaker describes his own positive feelings related to prior utterances of the other; for example, "Okay, now I understand what you are saying."

Confirmation and disconfirmation are assumed to occur in degrees. These degrees are represented by three levels of confirmation and three levels of disconfirmation.[13] These levels are hierarchical. Confirmation at level three implies confirmation at lower levels. With disconfirmation, the order of the levels is reversed. Level one disconfirmation is most extreme, with levels two and three being less extreme. The arrangement of confirming and disconfirming responses according to levels is presented in the accompanying table.

As was the case with Leary's category system, Sieburg's confirming

13Ibid., pp. 19–20.

and disconfirming categories are offered primarily because of the conceptual perspective they provide for understanding interpersonal processes in group communication. That group communication is frequently disjunctive and disconnected and fosters vague feelings of uneasiness and feelings that one is being disregarded or not sufficiently attended to, are among the most frequent complaints of group members. A basic understanding of confirming and disconfirming responses, and an opportunity

CONFIRMATION	DISCONFIRMATION

	ACKNOWLEDGMENT	IMPERVIOUSNESS
Level I	Looks at other while speaking; makes eye contact with him; gives attention without engaging in conversation with another person or performing other task. Speaks directly to other.	Looks away from other; avoids eye contact; ignores, pays no attention to other. Interrupts, speaks to another person, or performs other tasks while other is speaking; remains silent; makes no response when response seems appropriate; leaves the scene while other is speaking.

	A. CONJUNCTIVE RESPONSE (CONTENT)	DISJUNCTIVE RESPONSE
Level II	Comments relevantly to immediately preceding communication of other. Responds directly and on same subject as other. Provides unevasive answers to questions or expresses clear intent not to answer question ("I don't want to answer that."). B. CONJUNCTIVE RESPONSE (EMOTION) Comments relevantly about other's feelings; expresses own inferences about other's emotional state ("You sound angry to me."); clarifies other's feelings, expressed or inferred. Acknowledges other's emotions without evaluation of them.	Makes comment or interjection that is irrelevant to either the content of the preceding speaker's communication or his emotional state. Shifts to another topic without warning or explanation for shift. Other specific cases to be scored in this grouping: 1. Interrupts other. 2. Returns to own earlier theme, disregarding intervening interaction. 3. Responds tangentially by reacting to an incidental cue in other's communication, but missing main point. 4. Answers questions evasively or defensively. 5. Verbally denies other's expressed emotion ("You don't really feel that way."). 6. Negatively evaluates other's feelings by implying he ought not feel as he does.

	CONFIRMATION	DISCONFIRMATION

	AFFILIATIVE RESPONSE	DISAFFILIATIVE RESPONSE
	Discloses self to other in all of the following ways:	Conceals self or denies responsibility for his own communication in any of the following ways:
Level III	1. Speaks in complete and unfragmented sentences. Referents are obvious, words and expressions are used in commonly accepted ways; utterances are free of clichés and excessive verbiage; including unnecessary qualifiers and repetitive speech autom-isms (such as "you know").	1. Communication is obscure and hard to follow; sentences are fragmented, incomplete, rambling; speech is overloaded with automisms, overqualifications, retracings, rephrasings, and false starts. Referents are uncertain. Words or expressions have multiple meanings or seem to have meanings peculiar to the speaker.
	2. Expresses his own feelings freely and takes responsibility for them. Uses first person whenever appropriate in preference to the impersonal "one" or "you" or the generalized "we."	2. Speaker avoids expressing an emotion even in response to a direct question, or denies own emotion. Avoids personal construction substituting "one," "you," or a collective "we" when "I" seems more appropriate.
	3. Verbal message seems to agree with nonverbal modes; facial expression, body tone and gesture, tone of voice, and dress.	3. Verbal message does not seem consistent with nonverbal modes of voice tone, facial expression, body tone and gesture, or dress. Shows affect that is inappropriate to content.

Source: Evelyn Sieburg, "Toward a Theory of Interpersonal Confirmation" (unpublished ms., University of Denver, 1972). Reprinted by permission from Evelyn Sieburg.

to observe people's responses in group communication settings, may provide you with considerable insight into what should be considered one of the major distinguishable dimensions of communication.

V. *LEATHERS'S FEEDBACK RATING SCALES*

We suggest the use of Leathers's feedback rating scales in your observations of group communication phenomena for three reasons: (1) They provide a good illustration of rating scales, as contrasted with the use of category systems. (2) They represent a relatively recent development in group observation techniques. (3) Leathers's conceptual perspective is consistent with the increasing emphasis on a process-oriented approach to observing group communication phenomena, more specifically an emphasis on the analysis of communication in terms of sequences of contiguous communicative acts performed by group members.

The scales were developed originally for use in formal empirical investigations,[14] but more recently they have been proposed as useful in guiding the observation of classroom discussions.[15]

Groups, and group communication, vary considerably. Groups assume characteristics, distinguishing features, and unique forms much in the same way that individuals are characterized as possessing widely varying "personalities." In describing Sieburg's category system, we suggested that one of the basic dimensions along which group communication varies is in terms of the relative frequency of, and the levels of, confirming and disconfirming responses exhibited by group members. What gives group communication its particular flavor is the relatively consistent patterns with which members of a particular group respond to each other. Patterns of interpersonal responses distinguish effective from ineffective groups, functional from dysfunctional groups, pleasant from discomforting groups, and orderly from chaotic groups. Any truly complete description of the nature of communication must take into account the pattern of interpersonal responses.

Leathers's focus is upon *feedback events*. Feedback responses immediately follow, and are substantively related, to *stimulus statements*. Thus, feedback responses are linked in time and in content to other communicative acts and do not, by themselves, represent distinct breaks in the content of group discussion. The observational unit to be rated is usually a group member's complete utterance, immediately preceded and followed by utterances of another group member. The observational unit is considered a feedback response if it is substantively related to and directed toward the preceding utterance.

Of course, it would be extremely difficult for you, as an observer, to rate every individual feedback event in a group's interaction. Consequently, the feedback events to be rated are selected according to some predetermined strategy. For example, to obtain a sample of the feedback responses occurring in a group, every *n*th feedback response might be rated. To determine ways in which a particular group member is responded to, those feedback responses that immediately follow a particular member's contributions might be rated. Similarly, to determine particular

[14]Dale G. Leathers, "Process Disruption and Measurement in Group Communication," *Quarterly Journal of Speech* 55 (1969): 287–300.

[15]Dale G. Leathers, "The Feedback Rating Instrument: A New Means of Evaluating Discussion," *Central States Speech Journal* 22 (Spring 1971): 32–42.

members' patterns of feedback responsiveness, a given member's responses might be rated.

A given feedback response is rated along each of nine dimensions. The feedback rating instrument, including those nine dimensions, is represented in Figure 5–3.

In rating feedback responses, the observer first decides whether the plus or minus end of the scale is dominant. For example, scale number one rates the deliberateness of a feedback response. The observer first decides whether, generally, the response represents a deliberate or an automatic response. Having decided which end of the scale is dominant, the observer then rates the intensity (one, two, or three) of the response. Leathers has provided the following illustrative responses, one response for each end of each scale. These are responses to a stimulus statement concerning whether Hubert Humphrey can be fairly attacked for his alleged lack of liberalism:

Scale 1 (Symbol Response): "Give me a moment to think about that—I believe that we will have to formulate a careful definition of liberalism before I can give a thoughtful answer."

Scale 1 (Signal Response): "No! Absolutely not! Ridiculous! Humphrey is an extreme liberal. Nothing else."

Scale 2 (Relevant): "Harry, how does your point about Humphrey's civil rights background relate to the point Bob was making just before you spoke?"

Scale 2 (Irrelevant): "Humphrey's Southern strategy hasn't been discussed. Let's forget what we have been discussing and concentrate on that."

Scale 3 (Unified): "I believe Humphrey is the personification of the liberal because of his commitment to change, to the notion that man is basically good, and to the idea that group action is necessary to solve individual problems."

Scale 3 (Atomized): "Well certainly, Humphrey is a, that is to say: let me back up and start over. I believe Nixon, that is, Humphrey, to be. . . ."

Scale 4 (Clear): "Your definition of liberal seems particularly clear to me."

Scale 4 (Confused): "I have no idea of what you are talking about. Do you mean liberalism in the New Deal sense or the Burkean sense?"

Scale 5 (Relaxed *or* Tense): Responses which exhibit varying degrees of tension cannot be illustrated through verbal examples since the degree of tension in a given response is determined by nonverbal indicators.

Scale 6 (Ideational): "That indeed is a provocative thought which in turn raises two additional questions."

Scale 6 (Personal): "Frankly I think that is an asinine idea, Charles, and I don't see why a man of your alleged sophistication would bring it up."

Scale 7 (Flexible): "I had never considered the viewpoint which you just expressed. Let's consider it."

Scale 7 (Inflexible): "I am absolutely convinced that Hubert Humphrey is LBJ's sycophant. My view is clearly quite compelling so I see no need to consider your inference that Humphrey is his own man."

	+						−
Symbol			Deliberateness				Signal
3	2	1	0	1	2	3

Scale #1

Symbol response represents a deliberate, carefully reasoned, logical response; signal response represents an immediate, unthinking, largely automatic, visceral response of Y to X.

Relevant			Relevancy			Irrelevant
3	2	1	0	1	2	3

Scale #2

Relevancy—extent to which Y seeks to establish the connection between X's comment and the comment which immediately preceded X's comment.

Unified			Atomization			Atomized
3	2	1	0	1	2	3

Scale #3

Degree to which Y's contribution involves incomplete, fragmented or disjoined thought; includes running a number of ideas together; a number of people talking at the same time.

Clear			Fidelity			Confused
3	2	1	0	1	2	3

Scale #4

Extent to which Y's response to X exhibits confusion as to the meaning and/or intent of X's original message; characterized by the necessity of Y seeking clarification, definition, expansion, etc., from X.

Relaxed			Tension			Tense
3	2	1	0	1	2	3

Scale #5

Degree to which nonverbal gestures like laughter, sighs, groans, etc., indicate Y's relative state of tension or relaxation.

Ideational			Ideation			Personal
3	2	1	0	1	2	3

Scale #6

Ideational responses involve an appraisal or evaluation of X's ideas; personal responses represent the degree to which Y's comments involve direct or implied criticism of X as a person.

	Flexible			Flexibility			Inflexible
Scale #7	3	2	1	0	1	2	3

Inflexible response indicates Y's unwillingness to modify his position in response to X's contribution, may include a counter assertion.

	Concise			Digression			Digressive
Scale #8	3	2	1	0	1	2	3

Degree to which Y inhibits X's immediate response, primarily by means of lengthy and discursive utterances.

	Involved			Involvement			Withdrawn
Scale #9	3	2	1	0	1	2	3

Degree to which Y seeks to avoid comment on X's contribution by attempting to withdraw from the discussion of X's contribution.

FIGURE 5–3 Feedback rating instrument.

Source: From Dale G. Leathers, "The Feedback Rating Instrument: A New Means of Evaluating Discussion," *Central States Speech Journal*, 22 (Spring 1971): 32–42. Reprinted by permission of Dale G. Leathers and the Central States Speech Association.

Scale 8 (Concise): "Please amplify your suggestion, Harry."
Scale 8 (Digressive): "Before I can answer your question I'd like to spend the next few minutes tracing the history of liberalism." (The discussant then proceeds at great length almost as if he were a compulsive talker.)
Scale 9 (Involved): "Do you have a copy of Humphrey's voting record which we might examine?"
Scale 9 (Withdrawn): "What do you say we have a couple of beers before we discuss any more politics."[16]

As may be evident from the examples provided, the feedback rating instrument was originally employed to investigate the disruptive effects of certain types of stimulus statements on group communication processes. If, for example, you were interested in observing the effects of disagreement on group communication processes, you would rate only those feedback responses that follow instances in which group members express disagreement with the ideas, suggestions, or positions advanced by other group members.

[16]Ibid., p. 39. Reprinted by permission from Dale G. Leathers and the Central States Speech Association.

The five observation systems we have described are representative of those employed in the observation of group communication. It is common practice among group communication researchers to develop their own observation systems, category systems, or rating scales to meet particular research objectives. You may have observational objectives for which these five systems are inappropriate. You should be encouraged to experiment with the development and use of other observation systems. In a sense, this entire book provides guidelines for observing group communication. If you have encountered some notion about group communication that you would like to tentatively test through your own observations, you should be encouraged to do so. For many students and scholars, what makes group communication such an intriguing area of theory and research is the continual, and frequently pedestrian, process of developing methods for better understanding a very complicated phenomenon.

SUMMARY

1. Observation systems are methods for organizing and better understanding the complicated phenomenon of group communication.

2. There are two types of observation systems: category systems classify units or events according to preestablished categories; rating scales rate units along one or more continua.

3. Observation systems may be relatively more intellective (focusing on group communication behavior directed toward problem solving) or more interpersonal (focusing on communication behavior involved in developing and maintaining member feelings and sentiments).

4. The following observation systems are useful guides for evaluating ongoing group communication processes:

A. Functional roles—an intellective category system which arranges member participation into three member-role categories: group task roles, group building and maintenance roles, and individual roles. Each member may enact more than one role at any given time.

B. Bale's interaction process analysis—a system organized around twelve categories which provide information about both task and social-emotional behaviors and about the problem-solving phases through which a group progresses.

C. An early interpersonal system—Leary's category system that codes interpersonal behavior in terms of the motives inferred from those behaviors. The system focuses on the interpersonal mechanisms through which relationships are formed and maintained.

D. Sieburg's analysis of confirmation—a category system in which group communication is identified as functional or dysfunctional in terms of whether member communicative acts are "confirming" or "disconfirming."

E. Leathers's feedback rating scales—a rating scale system which emphasizes the analysis of communication in terms of sequences of contiguous communicative acts performed by group members. The scale helps to identify the group "personality."

5. Even when you use observation systems informally, it is useful and important to compare your observations with those of others.

leadership

6

After studying this chapter, you should be able to:

Trace the various approaches taken toward leadership in small groups.

State the differences between task and social-emotional behaviors as they apply to leadership function.

Describe how category systems and rating scales can be used to systematically describe leadership in a group.

Develop the perspective that group communication specialists presently are concerned more with inquiry than with the giving of advice.

Begin to understand several leadership theories or models and to use them to analyze leadership behavior of self and others in small groups.

Perceive the reciprocal effect of group communication on leadership and of leadership on group communication.

When speech communication specialists interested in discussion began to examine leadership processes in the small group, they were strongly influenced by their rhetorical tradition. Essentially, they saw small-group leadership as the behavior exhibited by the leader or chairman of a discussion group or committee. Their efforts consisted largely of giving advice, based upon sound rhetorical principles, on how to handle the discussion leadership role effectively. It was not until the early 1950s that the more scientific approach to leadership began to have a significant impact on the work of discussion specialists. And only recently have students of discussion who view group communication as a scholarly area of study in speech communication recognized their obligation to approach leadership in a distinctive manner, consistent with their interest not just in groups, per se, but in the *communication process* in small face-to-face groups.

This chapter on leadership is divided into three major sections. The first looks at group leadership as it has been approached traditionally by discussion specialists. The second section examines the implications of more scientific developments in the leadership area as reflected by the work of social scientists and practitioners identified with such fields and disciplines as social psychology, psychotherapy, and organizational development. The third and final section discusses the more specialized and distinctive leadership concerns of the contemporary group communication specialist.

The Rhetorical-Perspective Tradition

Some of the early specialists in group communication assumed that discussion invariably occurs under the direction of a leader and that a skilled leader can help group members considerably with their attempts at problem solving. The leader might have been elected or appointed to his position, his responsibilities might be temporary or permanent, and he might even have emerged as the leader through interaction without ever having been formally assigned the task. Nevertheless, it seemed apparent that most discussion groups have leaders and that these leaders should be competent. Furthermore, specialists in discussion could identify the competencies that discussion leaders ought to possess and they could suggest ways to develop them.

The leadership competencies of traditional concern to discussion specialists consist of understandings and abilities of a perceptual or cognitive nature as well as specific behavioral skills associated with group interaction. Perceptual or cognitive abilities that a leader should develop are often difficult to observe or measure. They consist of such skills as understanding people and having a sense of social responsibility. They also involve a variety of rhetorical and organizational abilities including skill in outlining, facility in the analysis and synthesis of problems, and the ability to use democratic procedures and to employ such problem-solving methods as the reflective thinking process.

On a behavioral level, traditional discussion specialists do something that, in a sense, is once again coming into vogue. They identify specific communicative acts that a discussion leader ought to perform so that he can lead a group more effectively. Many contemporary specialists in group communication are also interested in improving the skills of discussion leaders. However, the primary purpose of the contemporary group communication specialist in examining the message behavior of discussion group leaders and members is inquiry. He wants to better understand the communication process in small face-to-face groups. Nevertheless, traditionalists and their contemporary counterparts are both interested in identifying specific communication behaviors associated with leadership. The following section identifies many of the leadership behaviors traditionally associated with the discussion process.

COMMUNICATION BEHAVIOR
TRADITIONALLY ASSOCIATED WITH DISCUSSION LEADERSHIP

Traditionalists in discussion have described the techniques of leadership in a variety of ways. Most of the "category systems" are similar to one another. They deal largely with leader behaviors that will help a group to handle its task more effectively. The following list of leadership behaviors is a synthesis of many discussion texts.[1,2,3,4,5]

GOALS AND TECHNIQUES
OF DISCUSSION LEADERSHIP

   I. Getting the Discussion Started.
      A. Initiating the discussion is an important responsibility of the discussion leader. Here are some of the ways in which he can start a discussion:
         1. State the problem and its importance.
         2. Identify the purpose of the discussion and describe some of the factors and forces that brought the group members together.
         3. Describe some of the important issues the group members must resolve.
         4. Present an incident or a case that dramatizes the problem.
         5. Ask the group members a question.

---

[1]Rupert L. Cortright and George L. Hinds, *Creative Discussion* (New York: Macmillan, 1959).

[2]Laura Crowell, *Discussion: Method of Democracy* (Chicago: Scott Foresman, 1963).

[3]William S. Howell and Donald K. Smith, *Discussion* (New York: Macmillan, 1956).

[4]John W. Keltner, *Group Discussion Processes* (New York: Longmans, Green, 1957).

[5]James H. McBurney and Kenneth G. Hance, *Discussion in Human Affairs* (New York: Harper and Brothers, 1939).

   B. Discussion Leader's Goals when Initiating a Discussion:
      1. To impress the group members with the importance of the task.
      2. To inform the group members about the topic and its implications.
      3. To establish a positive climate for discussion.
      4. To encourage participation.
II. Maintaining the Discussion.
   A. The discussion leader has an obligation to see that the discussion focuses on the question and that it proceeds in a systematic and orderly fashion. Here are some of the techniques he can use to accomplish this:
      1. Follow a problem-saving pattern such as the reflective thinking process:
         a. Encourage the group members to define the problem, to delimit it, and to see that they agree on the interpretation of the problem.
         b. Analyze the problem by giving or asking for information about the history of the problem, its causes, effects, its implications, positions taken by various authorities, and the like.
         c. Give and/or ask for criteria or standards for evaluating possible solutions to the problem.
         d. Assist the group members in developing a list of possible solutions to the problem.
         e. Encourage the group members to discuss the proposed solutions and to select the best one.
      2. Provide summaries of the progress the group has made.
      3. Present ideas and encourage others to do so.
      4. Help the group make transitions from one step to the next.
      5. Judge the evidence, reasoning, and ideas presented.
      6. Encourage group members to evaluate their generalizations.
   B. Discussion Leader's Goals When Maintaining the Discussion:
      1. To keep the discussion systematic and orderly.
      2. To see that the group makes progress toward its goal.
      3. To prevent the group from getting sidetracked on irrelevant issues and topics.
      4. To encourage discussion that is meaningful and that has enough depth.
      5. To help the group develop sound ideas.
III. Making Sure that Important Matters are Considered and that Constructive Use is Made of Conflict.

A. A discussion leader has a special obligation to see that a group handles its task in a sound and thorough way. He should also see to it that when conflicts occur, as they inevitably will, the group profits from the clash instead of being hurt by it. The following techniques can be used by a leader to achieve these purposes:
   1. Ask questions about matters that the group members have overlooked or that they have examined superficially.
   2. Play the devil's advocate by opposing points of view the leader agrees with to ensure that those viewpoints are given careful consideration and can be defended.
   3. Explore the evidence and logic behind conflicting viewpoints.
   4. Cut off those arguments that have become futile and reject the use of scare words, acts designed merely to be disruptive, and other destructive behavior.
B. When he encourages the consideration of important matters and deals with conflict, the discussion leader has these goals:
   1. To see to it that full advantage is taken of the discussion process.
   2. To prevent abuse of the discussion process.
   3. To help the discussants maximize their individual and collective potentials for effective discussion.
   4. To help the group members maintain confidence in their group and in the discussion process.
   5. To help the group find the best possible solution to the problem under consideration.
IV. Bringing the Discussion to a Close.
   A. Leadership must be exerted not only to initiate a discussion, but also to bring it to a satisfactory conclusion. Several techniques for terminating a discussion are available to the leader. Here are some of them:
      1. Summarize the issues that were discussed by the group.
      2. Briefly review the steps the group went through and the problem-solving stage the group reached.
      3. Summarize the conclusions the group reached.
      4. State the amount of progress made by the group.
      5. Provide the group members with feedback about their performance thus far.
   B. The goals of the leader when he terminates a discussion are:
      1. To give the group members a feeling of closure.
      2. To enable the group members to see what they have accomplished.

3. To generate a positive feeling about the group's accomplishments.
4. To set the stage for the next meeting of the group if additional meetings are anticipated or needed.

Traditional approaches to discussion emphasize two broad leadership goals: to solve problems effectively and to help each group member maximize his potential as a discussant in an atmosphere that is positive and encouraging. Leaders are also admonished not to abuse their authority or power. McBurney and Hance, for example, stress that a leader should stimulate an awareness of the group problem, but not agitate. They also warn the leader to guide but not dominate, and to integrate the ideas of the participants without dictating to them.[6]

The study of discussion developed largely out of a humanistic tradition and, consequently, it emphasized idea development rather than interpersonal involvement. It also stressed prescriptions for performing properly and effectively rather than methods for scientifically studying discussion groups. But the interest the social scientist, psychotherapist, and other academicians and professionals had in the small group generated bodies of literature and activities that the discussion specialist could not ignore. The developments in the small-group area were so pervasive that the discussion specialist could not avoid them—and a growing number of them did not want to, because over the years discussion specialists were themselves becoming more scientific in their orientations. The next section of this chapter explores some of the "social scientific" developments in the leadership area that have influenced the discussion and group communication specialist.

Approaches to Leadership Study

THE TRAIT APPROACH

When social scientists first began to explore leadership behavior systematically, many of them assumed that leaders possess certain traits that differentiate them from nonleaders. Researchers felt that if they could identify those traits then in addition to increasing our understanding of leadership phenomena, their findings would strengthen leadership efforts by establishing the specific traits or characteristics would-be leaders ought to develop or improve upon. This assumption and the research activity it generated became known as the trait approach to leadership study.

[6]Ibid., pp. 231–58.

The trait approach to leadership seemed to make a great deal of sense and during the 1930s and 1940s many investigations were published that found significant differences between leaders and nonleaders. In his summary of fifteen of these studies, Stogdill[7] cited research that suggested that leaders exceed the average person in their group in intelligence, scholarship, dependability in exercising responsibilities, activity and social participation, socioeconomic status, sociability, initiative, persistence, knowing how to get things done, self-confidence, cooperativeness, popularity, adaptability, and verbal facility. But, as the list of leadership characteristics grew, the value of the entire effort seemed to diminish. It began to appear as if the list of traits associated with leaders would be endless and that some of the traits would be contradictory. Furthermore, the trait approach failed to take situational factors into consideration. Height and weight, for example, might be important traits for leaders on the football field, but these same characteristics might prevent someone from being a successful jockey or nursery school teacher.

One of the major problems associated with the trait approach was created by the requirement that a leadership trait researcher must first distinguish between leaders and nonleaders in order to determine how the two groups differ from one another. But identifying a leader is not always an easy task. Is the group leader the individual who occupies a given office? Is he the person who influences the group members most often? Is he the best-liked or most-respected member of the group? Or is the leader the individual with the most power? The trait approach did not provide acceptable theoretical answers to these questions. Problems associated with the definition of leadership and with the influence of situational factors on leadership phenomena resulted eventually in a shift away from the trait approach and toward the functional approach to leadership study.

THE FUNCTIONAL APPROACH

The functional approach to leadership accepts the fact that it is difficult to identify one particular group member as the group leader and it deals with that problem by shifting the concern from one individual called the leader to the behaviors that are exhibited by all of the group members. Those behaviors that guide, influence, direct, or control others are considered leadership functions,[8] and leadership functions can and often are provided by many members of a group, not just those who are labeled "leader."

[7]Ralph M. Stogdill, "Personal Factors Associated with Leadership," *Journal of Psychology* 25 (1948): 35–71.

[8]Dean C. Barnlund and Franklyn S. Haiman, *The Dynamics of Discussion* (Boston: Houghton Mifflin, 1960), pp. 275–79.

The functional approach to leadership was more attractive to many social scientists than the trait approach because it was, in a sense, more empirical—more descriptive of what actually occurred. Among other things, it enabled the social scientist to deal with those behaviors in a group that actually influenced others whether or not they were performed by the designated leader, and it provided the researcher with a more operational definition of leadership. The leader could be defined not on the basis of his title or designation, but by identifying those group members who engaged in leadership acts more often than others.

Since the functional approach requires the identification of those acts or behaviors in a group that are influential, it was necessary for investigators to develop classification systems that would enable them to distinguish between acts in a group that were influential and those that were not. Categories of behaviors that were generally influential became known as leadership functions.

What behaviors are typically designated as leadership functions? It depends, ultimately, on the category system or the rating scale that one selects. You have already examined, in the preceding chapter, one of the earlier category systems (that of Benne and Sheats) developed to identify functional roles of members and leaders. The following rating scale was developed by Barnlund and Haiman to evaluate leadership in groups. It differentiates among those behaviors or functions that influence the procedure group members follow, the thinking they engage in, and the interpersonal relations of the group members.

BARNLUND-HAIMAN LEADERSHIP RATING SCALE[9]

Instructions: This rating scale may be used to evaluate leadership in groups with or without official leaders. In the latter case (the leaderless group) use part A of each item only. When evaluating the actions of an official leader use parts A and B of each item on the scale.

INFLUENCE IN PROCEDURE

INITIATING DISCUSSION

A. 3	2	1	0	1	2	3
Group needed more help in getting started			Group got right amount of help		Group needed less help in getting started	

B. The quality of the introductory remarks was:

Excellent	Good	Adequate	Fair	Poor

[9] Ibid., pp. 401–4. Reprinted by permission of the publishers.

ORGANIZING GROUP THINKING

A. 3	2	1	0	1	2	3
Group needed more direction in thinking			Group got right amount of help		Group needed less direction in thinking	

B. If and when attempts were made to organize group thinking they were:

Excellent	Good	Adequate	Fair	Poor

CLARIFYING COMMUNICATION

A. 3	2	1	0	1	2	3
Group needed more help in clarifying communication			Group got right amount of help		Group needed less help in clarifying communication	

B. If and when attempts were made to clarify communication they were:

Excellent	Good	Adequate	Fair	Poor

SUMMARIZING AND VERBALIZING AGREEMENTS

A. 3	2	1	0	1	2	3
Group needed more help in summarizing and verbalizing agreements			Group got right amount of help		Group needed less help in summarizing and verbalizing .agreements	

B. If and when attempts were made to summarize and verbalize agreements they were:

Excellent	Good	Adequate	Fair	Poor

RESOLVING CONFLICT

A. 3	2	1	0	1	2	3
Group needed more help in resolving conflict			Group got right amount of help		Group needed less help in resolving conflict	

B. If and when attempts were made to resolve conflict they were:

Excellent	Good	Adequate	Fair	Poor

INFLUENCE IN CREATIVE AND CRITICAL THINKING

STIMULATING CRITICAL THINKING

A. 3	2	1	0	1	2	3

Group needed more stimulation in creative thinking	Group got right amount of help	Group needed less stimulation in creative thinking

B. If and when attempts were made to stimulate ideas they were:

Excellent	Good	Adequate	Fair	Poor

ENCOURAGING CRITICISM

A. 3	2	1	0	1	2	3

Group needed more encouragement to be critical	Group got right amount of help	Group needed less encouragement to be critical

B. If and when attempts were made to encourage criticism they were:

Excellent	Good	Adequate	Fair	Poor

BALANCING ABSTRACT AND CONCRETE THOUGHT

A. 3	2	1	0	1	2	3

Group needed more be more concrete	Group achieved proper balance	Group needed to be more abstract

B. If and when attempts were made to balance abstract and concrete thought they were:

Excellent	Good	Adequate	Fair	Poor

INFLUENCE IN INTERPERSONAL RELATIONS

CLIMATE-MAKING

A. 3	2	1	0	1	2	3

Group needed more help in securing a permissive atmosphere	Group got right amount of help	Group needed less help in securing a permissive atmosphere

B. If and when attempts were made to establish a permissive atmosphere they were:

Excellent	Good	Adequate	Fair	Poor

REGULATING PARTICIPATION

A. 3	2	1	0	1	2	3
Group needed more regulation of participation			Group got right amount of help		Group needed less regulation of participation	

B. If and when attempts were made to regulate participation they were:

Excellent	Good	Adequate	Fair	Poor

OVERALL LEADERSHIP

A. 3	2	1	0	1	2	3
Group needed more control			Group got right amount of control		Group needed less control	

B. If and when attempts were made to control the group they were:

Excellent	Good	Adequate	Fair	Poor

The Barnlund and Haiman Leadership Rating Scale represents just one way of classifying leadership behavior in a group. A number of rating scales or alternative category systems are available. The Barnlund and Haiman scale, however, is characteristic of many others in the distinction it makes between procedural and task functions and interpersonal or process functions. The distinction between task and process is found throughout the small-group literature. It is referred to as attainment versus group maintenance,[10] as the external system versus the internal system,[11] as task versus social-emotional,[12] and in a number of other ways. The labels that are used to identify the two categories of behavior are less important than the distinction that is made between the two.

Task leadership behaviors are those that influence the goal-directed behavior of a group. Process leadership behaviors are those that assist the group members with their interpersonal relations and with the feelings they have about themselves, the situation, and one another. Research by Bales[13] and others indicates that individuals who provide task leadership functions in a group seldom provide process functions.

[10]Raymond B. Cattell, "Concept and Methods in the Measurement of Group Syntality," *Psychological Review* 55 (1948): 48–63.

[11]George C. Homans, *The Human Group* (New York: Harcourt, Brace and World, 1950).

[12]Robert F. Bales, *Interaction Process Analysis: A Method for the Study of Small Groups* (Cambridge, Mass.: Addison-Wesley, 1950).

[13]Robert F. Bales, "The Equilibrium Problem in Small Groups," in *Working Papers in the Theory of Action*, ed. T. Parsons, R. F. Bales, and E. A. Shils (Glencoe, Ill.: The Free Press, 1953), pp. 111–61.

Hence, a distinction can often be made between the task leadership structure and the process leadership structure in a group. Subsequent research by Marcus[14] and Turk[15] suggests that in at least some situations task process leadership may be provided by the same individual or group of individuals. Much seems to depend on the nature of the group task.

By using a category system or rating scale to determine the different kinds of leadership functions that are provided by members during a group session and by noting who provided them, it is possible systematically to describe leadership phenomena in a group. If leadership functions in a group, for example, are provided by many members, it could be said that the group's leadership is distributed as opposed to being in the hands of one person or a few. Insight can also be obtained into the kinds of leadership behavior that occurred, who provided what functions, the amount of time devoted to task versus process, and the changes in leadership phenomena that occurred during the group session.

In addition to its analytical and scientific value, the functional approach to leadership is attractive to group communication specialists because of its implications for leadership training. It is often easier and more reasonable to train group members to provide certain leadership functions in a group, such as asking for opinions or giving suggestions, than it is to assist them with the development of such traits or characteristics as self-confidence or intelligence. And many traits such as height or socioeconomic status are difficult if not impossible to do anything about. Research by Barnlund[16] demonstrated quite convincingly that an individual's group leadership ability could be improved significantly by using a training procedure based upon the functional approach.

LEADERSHIP STYLES

In the previous section we pointed out that leadership behaviors typically have been divided by social scientists into task and process categories and that the individuals who exhibit task leadership behaviors in a group are seldom the same individuals who provide process leadership functions. But if leadership behaviors can be described as functions and divided into task and process categories, they can be described and associated with different group members in other ways as well. One of

14P. M. Marcus, "Expressive and Instrumental Groups: Toward a Theory of Group Structure," *American Journal of Sociology* 66 (1960): 54–59.

15H. Turk, "Instrumental and Expressive Ratings Reconsidered," *Sociometry* 24 (1961): 76–81.

16Dean C. Barnlund, "Experiments in Leadership Training for Decision-Making Discussion Groups," *Speech Monographs* 22 (1955): 1–14.

these additional ways of classifying and generalizing about leadership behaviors was stimulated by Lewin and his associates during the 1930s.

Lewin and his associates, Ronald Lippitt and Ralph White,[17] were interested in determining if certain clusters of leadership behavior that seem to go together and that reflect certain philosophical positions or assumptions about the nature of man would have differential effects on a group. They labeled these different clusters of behavior "leadership styles" and examined the effects of three different styles on the social climate and productivity of groups of ten-year-old boys who met after school for hobby activities. Lewin and his associates described the three leadership styles they investigated as authoritarian, democratic, and laissez faire. The group communication specialist is interested in leadership styles because, among other things, they represent a way of classifying and characterizing a large number of communication behaviors that leaders engage in.

Laissez Faire Leadership

Laissez faire leadership refers essentially to a pattern of abrogation where the nominal leader or authority figure in a group tries to deny any serious responsibility for his followers. The adults who served as laissez faire leaders in the Lewin research avoided participation and maintained an attitude of indifference toward the youngsters in their group. They supplied materials and information only when asked and made comments of praise and criticism either infrequently or not at all.

Laissez faire leadership has not received as much attention over the years as the authoritarian and democratic styles described and investigated by Lewin, Lippitt, and White. "Authoritarian" and "democratic" represent opposite ends of the leadership style continuum, and they are the styles more commonly referred to when leadership patterns are discussed.

Authoritarian Leadership

Authoritarian leadership, according to Gordon,[18] is likely to reflect a negative, pessimistic, discouraging view of man. The authoritarian leaders in the Lewin, Lippitt, and White research exploited their followers' dependency needs by determining group policy without consult-

---

[17]Kurt Lewin, Ronald Lippitt, and Ralph K. White, "Patterns of Aggressive Behavior in Experimentally Created 'Social Climates,'" *Journal of Social Psychology* 10 (1939): 271–99.

[18]Thomas Gordon, *Group-Centered Leadership* (Boston: Houghton Mifflin, 1955).

ing the group members, by dictating group tasks and setting forth procedures for accomplishing them, by subjectively praising and criticizing the group members, and by maintaining an impersonal and aloof attitude. Communication in the group occurred primarily through the leader; members were discouraged from communicating directly with each other.

Democratic Leadership

The democratic leader's view of man is much more optimistic and positive than the view held by the authoritarian leader. He sees man as capable of self-direction and attempts to provide his followers with the opportunity for growth, development, and self-actualization. In the Lewin, Lippitt, and White research, the democratic leader facilitated communication among group members by encouraging them to determine group policy and activities. He did this by suggesting alternative goals and procedures, by allowing the group members to choose their own work partners, by objectively praising and criticizing the youngsters, and by soliciting suggestions. It is important to note that the democratic leaders did not necessarily exert less power than the authoritarian leaders. They merely used that power to spread rather than restrict responsibility and to encourage mutual support and respect rather than distrust and suspicion among group members.

Nondirective Leadership

Occasionally, the democratic leadership style studied by Lewin and his associates is confused with nondirective leadership. There is an obvious overlap between the two styles, but they are distinguishable, nevertheless. Like the democratic leader, the nondirective leader avoids dominating the group and encourages the group members to assume more responsibility. The nondirective leader does this, however, by communicating with other group members in the way Rogers recommends that a client-centered therapist should communicate with his clients.[19] Instead of overtly controlling or influencing the group members, the nondirective leader tries to understand what the group members are thinking and feeling so that he can reflect back that understanding. By refusing to give the group direction, the nondirective leader allows the group to determine its own goals and to assume its own responsibility for achieving them. The group members may experience a great deal of pain and agony when they fail to receive direction from their "authority figure," but the assumption is that as long as the nondirective leader

[19]Carl Rogers, *Client-Centered Thearpy* (Boston: Houghton Mifflin, 1951).

really and truly cares about the group and reflects that concern and caring back to the group members, the pain associated with not receiving direction from the leader will result ultimately in greater group growth and maturity.

The Lewin, Lippit, and White research findings and the writings of Rogers and Gordon in the nondirective leadership area are often used by advocates of democratic or nondirective leadership to support their point of view. Although one could question the generalizability of results that are based upon the study of ten-year-old boys, the Lewin, Lippitt, and White research data do suggest rather strongly that at least under certain circumstances, and assuming that one values certain outcomes, a democratic style of leadership may be worthwhile. But it is important to recognize the difference between concluding that a particular leadership style is best under certain circumstances and becoming an advocate of that style.

The primary concern of the group communication specialist is inquiry, not advocacy, even though there are times when leadership styles or procedures must be ranked and a stand must be taken. One of the dangers associated with advocating a particular leadership strategy is the possibility that it will not work well in the situation for which it is being prescribed. A growing awareness of this fact resulted in the development of the situational approach to leadership and this is the approach that we examine in the following section.

THE SITUATIONAL APPROACH

The work of Lewin and his associates stimulated a great deal of interest in leadership styles that has persisted over the years. Research in this area by Preston and Heintz,[20] Gordon,[21] Selvin,[22] Likert,[23] and others has tended to confirm the generalization that group members are likely to be more satisfied and productive under conditions that involve leadership behaviors more closely associated with democratic than with authoritarian or laissez faire patterns. However, Lewin also influenced the development of the situational approach to leadership study, an approach that during the past decade or so has required a careful reexamination and reinterpretation of the leadership style literature.[24]

---

[20]M. G. Preston and R. K. Heintz, "Effects of Participatory vs. Supervisory Leadership on Group Judgment," *Journal of Abnormal and Social Psychology* 44 (1949): 345–55.

[21]Gordon, *Group-Centered Leadership.*

[22]H. C. Selvin, *The Effects of Leadership* (New York: The Free Press, 1960).

[23]Rensis Likert, *New Patterns of Management* (New York: McGraw-Hill, 1961).

[24]Edwin P. Hollander and James W. Julian, "Contemporary Trends in the Analysis of Leadership Processes," *Psychological Bulletin* 71, no. 5 (1969): 387–97.

The situational approach to leadership suggests that the effectiveness of a set of leadership traits, of a leadership style, or of particular leadership behaviors or functions can best be understood by carefully examining the context within which they occur. The situational approach to leadership[25],[26] grew out of an increasing awareness that the leadership position in a group could not be viewed as a homogeneous role[27] that cut across various group situations or that was independent of such factors as leader and follower perceptions and relationships. This viewpoint was strengthened by studies which clearly demonstrated that who becomes the leader in a group often depends on the nature of the group's task.[28] Furthermore, the leadership style an individual decides to use is significantly influenced by his perceptions regarding the status and credibility of his subordinates.[29] It was also reinforced by findings that the personality of group members influences the leadership style the group members prefer[30] as well as member satisfaction with their group experience.[31]

According to the "situationalists," to understand leadership phenomena one must take into account the relationships that exist among the group leader or leaders, their followers, and the situation they are in. The situation includes such factors as the size of the group, the group task, the way the group is structured, the norms of the group, the resources of every group member, and the group's history.

The importance of the situation in determining leadership behavior and effectiveness is further supported by the research findings related to the effects on productivity and decision making of different communication nets or networks. The study of communication nets began with Bavelas.[32] Bavelas developed a strategy for controlling the communication between members of a group by restricting the group members to written notes or printed materials and by limiting them to certain communication channels. Some of the channel or network arrangements used

[25]J. K. Hemphill, *Situational Factors in Leadership* (Columbia, Ohio: Ohio State University, Bureau of Educational Research, 1949).

[26]A. W. Gouldner, ed., *Studies in Leadership* (New York: Harper and Brothers, 1950).

[27]Hollander and Julian, "Analysis of Leadership Processes," p. 387.

[28]Ibid., p. 388.

[29]Alvin Goldberg, Lloyd Crisp, Evelyn Sieburg, and Michele Tolela, "Subordinate Ethos and Leadership Attitudes," *Quarterly Journal of Speech* 53 (1967): 354–60.

[30]F. H. Sanford, *Authoritarianism and Leadership* (Philadelphia: Institute of Research in Human Relations, 1950).

[31]Louis Lerea and Alvin Goldberg, "The Effects of Socialization Upon Group Behavior," *Speech Monographs* 28 (1961): 60–64.

[32]Alex Bavelas, "Communication Patterns in Task-Oriented Groups," *Journal of the Acoustical Society of America* 22 (1950): 725–30.

by Bavelas and other researchers are depicted in Figure 6–1.[33] Among other things, the network research demonstrated that the arrangement of channels was not the only factor that affected the structure of a group. Outcomes were determined by the nature of the group task, the number of decisions that the group members were asked to make, the communi-

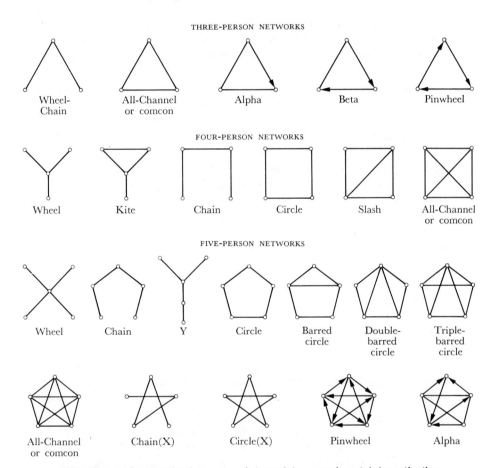

FIGURE 6–1 Communication networks used in experimental investigations. Dots represent positions, lines represent communication channels, and arrows indicate one-way channels.

Source: From Marvin E. Shaw, "Communication Networks," in *Advances in Experimental Social Psychology*, vol. 1, ed. Leonard Berkowitz (New York: Academic Press, 1964), p. 113. Reprinted by permission of Marvin E. Shaw and Academic Press, Inc.

[33]Marvin E. Shaw, "Communication Networks," in *Advances in Experimental Social Psychology*, vol. 1, ed. Leonard Berkowitz (New York: Academic Press, 1964), pp. 111–47.

cation network that the group members were previously in, and a number of other factors in addition to channel arrangement. To understand the performance of a group in a particular communication network, many *situational* factors had to be considered.

Over the years, then, social scientists have moved from a relatively simple search for leadership traits, description of leadership functions, or examination of leadership styles, to a relatively more sophisticated situational approach to leadership that recognizes the interaction among the various forces and factors that influence leadership processes. As Burke once put it, "to designate particular types of behavior as leadership behavior is as absurd as to designate particular personality traits as leader traits . . . it's not just the behaviors . . . it's the normative expectations of the group members about these."[34] Situationalists might add that group size, group norms and traditions, and many other factors in addition to member expectations are likely to determine whether or not particular acts should be identified as leadership behaviors.

In our focus on some of the social scientific literature dealing with leadership we have considered the trait, functional, and situational approaches to leadership study, and we have examined some of the research that has been conducted in the area of leadership styles. We now turn briefly to three theories that have been developed to explain leadership events.

Theories of Leadership

A BEHAVIORAL MODEL

Bass[35] views leadership from a behavioral point of view. According to Bass, individuals join groups to obtain rewards or to avoid punishment. If barriers to reward attainment are encountered, some group members will try to do something about the matter; they will attempt to change the behavior of others. Bass defines these acts as *attempted leadership.* If others actually change as a result of these attempts, the acts become *successful leadership.* If the group is rewarded because of these changes, the influence attempts are referred to by Bass as *effective leadership.* The amount of attempted, successful, and effective leadership that occurs in a group, according to Bass, is a function of the group's attractiveness and the amount of esteem the group members have for one another.

Bass suggests that the group members who are most likely to attempt

---

[34]P. J. Burke, "Authority Relations and Descriptive Behavior in Small Discussion Groups," *Sociometry* 29 (1966): 250.

[35]Bernard M. Bass, *Leadership, Psychology, and Organizational Behavior* (New York: Harper and Brothers, 1960).

leadership are those individuals with higher self-esteem and those who were successful leaders in previous sessions. Previously effective members are also most likely to succeed in their influence attempts.

The most effective leaders will be those who are capable of dealing with the group's problems. A leader's success will be influenced by the perceptions of the other group members. If the other group members view the situation as one in which the individual attempting leadership is effective, he is more likely to succeed. The power a person has (which may be derived from his status and esteem), as well as his ability to persuade, will also determine the success of his influence attempt.

A CONTINGENCY MODEL

The contingency model of leadership effectiveness was developed by Fiedler.[36] The model and the research data upon which it is based support the situational approach to leadership discussed earlier in this chapter. In general, the Fiedler theoretical model assumes that an appointed or elected leader's effectiveness will be determined largely by how favorable the group situation is for him. "Favorableness" depends upon such factors as the group task, the power position of the leader, and the type of relationship that exists between the leader and the other group members. Fiedler defines leader effectiveness as the success of the leader's group in achieving its goals.

Fiedler's major concern is the effectiveness of two different leadership styles: psychologically distant and controlling versus a more permissive and psychologically close style. The distant and controlling style is similar to the autocratic patterns studied by Lewin, Lippitt, and White, and the psychologically close or permissive style is similar to the democratic pattern that Lewin and his associates examined. When Fiedler first began his investigations, he hypothesized that the more autocratic or distant leaders would be less effective than the more close or permissive leaders. But his data supported just the opposite relationship. Subsequent research revealed that the relationship between leadership style and leadership effectiveness depends upon the leader's relationship with the group members, the group task, and the power of the leader.

According to the Fiedler model, the leader-group relationship is most favorable when the leader is respected and liked. A liking relationship enables the leader to be more decisive and to obtain the cooperation of the group members without resorting to power. The group task situation is most favorable when it is clear and unambiguous. Confusion

---

[36]Fred E. Fiedler, *A Theory of Leadership Effectiveness* (New York: McGraw-Hill, 1967).

over goals and how they can be reached is highly unfavorable. The leader's power position is most favorable when he has the strong support of the larger organization or authority and when the leader has control over various forms of reward and punishment. The relationship between the leader and the group is the most important of the three factors and the leader's power is the least important.

According to the Fiedler model, the effectiveness of a leadership style is a function of the favorableness of the situation. If the group task is clear and unambiguous, if the leader enjoys a good relationship with the group members, and if the leader has power, a controlling or autocratic style will be most effective. A controlling or autocratic style will also be most likely to result in group goal achievement when the situation is highly unfavorable. But when the situation is not at either extreme and, instead, is moderately favorable or moderately unfavorable, the Fiedler theoretical model, which is supported by solid research data, calls for a more permissive and more democratic leadership style.

AN INTERPERSONAL MODEL

A third and final leadership model is provided by Schutz.[37] The model is based upon some of the explorations that Schutz conducted in the area of interpersonal needs. Schutz was concerned with, among other things, the compatibility of group members who have different need systems.

The three basic categories that Schutz developed to classify interpersonal needs emerge from a psychoanalytic base. They consist of the need for inclusion (superego), for control (ego), and for affection (id). Inclusion refers to the need to maintain satisfactory relationships with others and to have a sufficient amount of involvement and belongingness. Control is associated with the need for power and influence. Affection refers to the need for love, friendship, and closeness. Schutz points out that every individual's interpersonal needs are different. Some prefer to control others, some prefer to be controlled, and most individuals are probably someplace in the middle of the control continuum. The same differences between people are found on the other two interpersonal need dimensions.

The interpersonal needs of group members are related to the leadership process in groups because of the influence they can have on that process. If the interpersonal needs of the group members are not satisfied or incompatible, the leadership attempts designed to assist the

---

[37]William C. Schutz, *FIRO (Fundamental Interpersonal Relations Orientation): A Three Dimensional Theory of Interpersonal Behavior* (New York: Rinehart, 1958).

group in achieving its task may fail. A group that contains too many members with high control needs may find itself engaged in a destructive leadership struggle, and a group with too many low inclusion members may not respond well to leadership attempts.

Schutz suggests that to be successful, a leader must help group members satisfy their interpersonal needs both in their interaction with one another and in their collective involvement with their environment. Individual group members, for example, must have enough inclusion to satisfy their need to be part of things, but not so much that they lose their autonomy or have to change their life styles. As a group, they must become involved enough with external events to maintain their status in the community, but not so involved that they lose their group identity or integrity. To be effective, similar member and group balances should be sought by the group's leadership in the interpersonal need areas of control and affection.

Although the Schutz model suggests that the leader of a group should seek an appropriate external and internal balance for the group members and the group as a whole in the three interpersonal areas, Schutz does not believe that the leader or leaders of a group must achieve these goals alone. A leader should see to it that his group's needs are met, but they can be met by any of the group members, not just the leader. Schutz's views with regard to this matter, which he describes as "leader as completer," is similar to a position taken by Haiman.[38] Haiman believes that a leader should perform the leadership functions in a group if no one else does, but that a good leader is one who works his way out of a job.

THE MINNESOTA STUDIES

Some of the most significant speech communication research in the leadership area has been conducted under the direction of Bormann at the University of Minnesota. The body of research that Professor Bormann directed has become known as the Minnesota Studies. A number of these studies are summarized by Bormann in his text entitled *Discussion and Group Methods*.[39]

Bormann and his associates defined leadership on the basis of the perceptions of group members. In the Minnesota research the leader of a group is the individual who eventually was perceived as leader by all

[38]Franklyn S. Haiman, "Discussion Leader—Man, Not Superman," *Adult Leadership*, 1 (1953) pp. 5–7.

[39]Ernest G. Bormann, *Discussion and Group Methods* (New York: Harper & Row, 1969), pp. 200–224.

of the group members, including the person designated as leader. The role of the leader was observed and analyzed by carefully studying groups of strangers who were given no formal structure, but who were given a specific task to work on and a time limit for its completion. The basic data-gathering model was referred to as to the **LGD** or *leaderless group discussion.*

The Minnesota studies indicate that after a few hours of discussion, most groups develop some sort of structure. Members begin to differentiate themselves on the basis of status and esteem. Members also become distinguishable in terms of the functions they serve in the group. But functions are not assumed in an arbitrary manner. They have to be negotiated. Members who engage in certain acts are either encouraged or discouraged to continue those acts by the responses they receive from the other group members. The responses a member receives are, to some extent, a function of the phase the group is in. Behaviors that are appropriate during one time period are not necessarily appropriate during another period.

Once some sort of role structure is established, the group members distinguish between these roles in terms of importance; these status distinctions are directly related to our concern in this chapter with leadership and group communication. The individual who emerges as a leader in a group is the individual who has been able to receive positive reinforcement for his leadership attempts from the other group members. The leader secures this role through a process of negotiation with the other group members, and the negotiations are seldom similar from one group to the next. Hence, leadership in a group is somewhat idiosyncratic. It depends partially, at least, on the negotiations that take place in any particular group.

The Minnesota studies indicate that group members with high esteem needs are likely to enter into a leadership struggle early in a group's existence, and in most but not all groups a leader eventually emerges. According to Bormann, a group "selects its leader by the method of residues."[40] Instead of selecting a leader, groups eliminate individuals from contention until only one is left. Quiet members, or those whose communications cause them to be perceived as not being intelligent or well informed are dropped first. Aggressive communicators who appear to be too rigid and unequivocal are also rejected quickly in most instances. About half the group members remain in contention for the leadership role when the group enters a *second phase.*

Phase two is a tense and difficult one. Members are irritated with one another and the competition is stiff. Individuals are dropped from

[40]Ibid., p. 207.

contention for the leadership role on the basis of sex, leadership style, inflexibility, and a variety of other criteria. Finally, one individual is left and this person is acknowledged by the members as the group leader. Bormann identifies four "archetypal" patterns within this general pattern. Pattern one consists of a situation where two contenders are left. One contender obtains a strong lieutenant and the other does not. The contender with a lieutenant becomes the leader. In pattern two a number of final contenders obtain lieutenants. A leader never emerges from some groups that fall into a number two pattern. Pattern three is one where a crisis develops. The individual who demonstrates that he can best handle that crisis obtains the leadership role. The fourth and final pattern is one where no member clearly emerges as the leader.

The Minnesota Studies are primarily descriptive in nature. They required a great deal of observation and systematic analysis. By carefully observing, recording, and analyzing the communication behavior of leaderless groups (that is, of groups without designated leaders), the investigators were able to obtain worthwhile insights into the emergence of leadership in initially unstructured groups. Additional descriptive research of this nature, as well as experimental studies designed to test hypotheses derived from propositions suggested either by the Minnesota Studies, by the various leadership theories presented in this chapter, or by new leadership theories developed by group communication specialists, will help in the development of group communication as an area of scholarship in speech communication.

SUMMARY

1. Traditional approaches emphasize two broad leadership goals: (1) to solve problems effectively; (2) to help each group member maximize his potential as a discussant in an atmosphere that is positive and encouraging. Idea development is stressed rather than interpersonal involvement. Prescriptions for improving leadership skills and effectiveness are stressed rather than methods for scientifically studying discussion groups.

2. Group communication specialists, in contrast to discussion specialists, are primarily interested in leadership as an area of inquiry.

3. Social scientists have taken several approaches toward leadership:

A. The trait approach was first and was based on the assumption that leaders possess certain traits that differentiate them from others.

B. The functional approach shifted the concern from one individual called the leader to the behaviors that are exhibited by all of the group members; such behaviors are considered leadership functions and are provided by many members of a group, not just those labeled "leader." Barnlund and Haiman developed one rating scale to evaluate leadership in groups according to those behaviors or functions that influence the procedure groups follow, the thinking they engage in, and the interpersonal relations of the group members.

C. The situational approach suggests that the effectiveness of a particular leadership style depends on the context or situation within which that style will be used. To understand leadership phenomena, one must consider the relationships that exist among the group leader or leaders, their followers, and the situation they are in (situation includes size of group, task, group structure, group norms, resources of members, etc.).

4. Group communication specialists are interested in leadership style because it represents a way of classifying a large number of communication behaviors that leaders engage in. Leadership style classifications include:

A. Laissez faire leadership—a pattern of abrogation where the nominal leader tries to deny any responsibility for his followers.

B. Authoritarian leadership—member participation is discouraged in favor of the leader dictating all procedures and tasks; the leader here exploits his followers dependency needs and attempts to maintain complete control.

C. Democratic leadership—a pattern which views man as capable of self-direction and attempts to provide members with opportunities for growth, development, and self-actualization through participation in the control of themselves.

D. Nondirective leadership—the leader refuses to give the group direction and tries instead to understand what the group members are thinking and feeling so that he can reflect back that understanding. The group thus assumes responsibility for determining and achieving its own goals.

5. Several theories and models attempt to explain leadership events:
A. The Bass behavioral model suggests circumstances that lead to some member or members assuming leadership functions and suggests what makes for successful or effective leadership.

B. The Fiedler contingency model attempts to explain which leadership style is most appropriate for which situation and why.

C. The Schutz interpersonal model suggests that a successful leader must help group members satisfy their interpersonal needs in the areas of inclusion, control, and affection, both in their collective involvement with their environment and in their interaction with one another. The leader alone is, however, not solely responsible for achieving these goals.

6. The Minnesota Studies provide information on the definition of leadership, the process through which "leaderless" groups pass in their attempts to select a leader, the characteristics of those vying for leadership, and the differences that are evident in the process during various phases of group development.

group communication
for
problem solving

7

OBJECTIVES

After studying this chapter, you should be able to:

Improve your performance in problem-solving groups by taking into account several factors which inhibit or enhance effective group problem solving.

Gain insight into the alternative processes operating in problem-solving or decision-making groups.

Differentiate between several systematic methods for analyzing problems.

Dispel the accuracy myth with the more useful contention that solutions are either adequate or inadequate (i.e., how defensible a judgment is when confronted by opposing points of view).

Somewhere, at this very moment, a group of individuals is meeting for the expressed purpose of solving a problem or making a decision which will have a direct effect on you. The group may be a legislative committee at the local, state, or federal level, and its decisions may determine whether a certain piece of land will be made available for your recreational activities, or whether you will be able to drive southward on Birchwood Street, or whether you will be confronted by certain hiring and employment policies at some future time. Countless other decisions are currently being made for you by people in small groups. Curriculum decisions, degree requirements, faculty staffing, and other decisions are being considered, and deliberations are in progress or are being planned. These decisions include the kinds of entertainment you will be offered, the restaurants you may select from, the cost of your new automobile license tags, and so on, and on, and on.

Perhaps with just a little effort, you may appreciate the extent to which small-group problem solving and decision making permeate our lives and the extent to which society and its institutions rely on one basic process: small groups interacting for purposes of solving problems and making decisions. The basic group communication processes operating in the small city council are much the same as those that operate within the Cabinet of the United States. Indeed, Janis has analyzed group processes in executive decisions surrounding Viet Nam, the Bay of Pigs, Korea, and Pearl Harbor. Janis has identified characteristics of groups involved in making the decisions which led to these fiascos.[1] We would probably recognize these same characteristics as describing many of the small groups in which we have participated.

That we know so little about a process on which we rely so much is disquieting. That most of us have acquired some experience in dealing with group phenomena is of little comfort. If experience were sufficient to improve group communication processes, we would all be better participants than we tend to be, and group problem-solving and decision-making deliberations would be far less chaotic and frustrating. If group communication is to be improved, our experience must be accompanied by some insight into the processes operating, as well as some conceptual and behavioral alternatives.

Accuracy versus Adequacy

Understanding the basic group problem-solving strategy requires that we dispel a myth surrounding group problem-solving activities. The myth is that problem solutions are either right or wrong. People and groups frequently approach problem situations with the belief that their task is to "solve the problem correctly" or to "make the right decision." Most problems that confront individuals and groups, however, are not the kinds of problems for which there are accurate or inaccurate solutions. This is especially true of problems that confront groups; indeed, problems with "absolute" solutions are seldom brought to groups for deliberation. If there is a right or wrong answer to a problem, then the

[1]Irving L. Janis, "Groupthink," *Psychology Today* 5 (November 1971): 43 et passim.

process of discovering the right answer ordinarily consists of doing some research, or looking up the facts.

The "accurary" myth is a difficult one to dispel. Much of the research on group problem solving, including some of our own, implicitly assumes that the task of groups is to discover the correct solution to a problem. The problems, particularly the kinds of problems that confront groups, rarely have "correct" solutions or right and wrong answers. Consider, for example, the following illustrative cases in which we have been directly involved. These are not hypothetical cases, nor are they the most difficult or complicated problems we can remember being involved in.

1. Officers of a large service industry contacted a team of evaluation researchers. The researchers were asked to "evaluate" a management institute. The management institute was offered once a year, for one week, by an agency of a large midwestern university. The service industry paid the bills, and its officers were beginning to wonder whether they were getting their money's worth. The participants in the institute were drawn from a variety of levels and positions in the industry. The industry kept no record and gathered no data specifically relevant to the question of whether job performance characteristics of the participants changed as a function of their attendance at the institute. Officers of the industry, including those responsible for the management institute, had no formal statement of goals or objectives for the institute.

2. Before fair housing legislation was enacted in a certain state, a community human relations commission was asked to "handle" a case involving alleged racial discrimination. Two black renters contended that the owner of a four-unit apartment house was attempting to evict them because they were black. The renters stated that they had arranged by telephone to rent an apartment advertised in the local paper. On the day that the renters delivered their check for the first month's rent and picked up the key to the apartment from the owner, they claimed that the owner "seemed surprised" that they were black. One week later, the renters were served notice by registered mail that the owner was starting eviction proceedings and that they had one month to vacate the apartment. They phoned the owner to ask why they were being evicted, but the owner replied that his attorney had advised him not to discuss the case. Preliminary investigations by the human relations commission disclosed: (1) The owner and his attorney, in conference with the commission, claimed absolutely no discriminatory basis for asking the renters to move. (2) The owner showed the commission a note from one of his renters in the apartment units; the person complained that the black renters had staged "a wild party the night they moved in, with people tramping up and down the stairs until one A.M. and noise like a wild orgy or something." (3) The black renters claimed not to have had a wild or noisy party. They stated that on the night in question they had asked two of their friends over and that they had watched television and played cards

until 12:30 A.M. (4) The complaining renter refused to talk to the commission; he stated that he did not want to be bothered by a lot of "silly" questions. (5) The owner stated that the complaining renter was an older retired man who had been renting his apartment for 14 years. (6) The only other occupant of the apartment building who was home the night in question stated that she had heard the renters "laughing" late in the evening, but did not consider it "excessive noise."

3. The board of directors of a property owners association holds an annual meeting. The membership of the organization consists of individuals who own property in a given land development. There are approximately 500 members of the property owners association. Each of the members has paid his annual dues. The constitution of the association requires that a specific proportion of the annual dues be spent making improvements in the land development for the general benefit of the membership at large. The board of directors is empowered to make decisions concerning the distribution of income generated by yearly membership dues. The constitution of the property owners association does not specify the types of improvements to be made.

If you approach such problem situations expecting to find the "right" answer, you will inevitably be somewhat disappointed in your ability to do so. Furthermore, if you believe that you have arrived at a "correct" solution, you must experience considerable frustration when you encounter other individuals whose solutions differ from yours. We will assume that your experiences have brought you to the realization that problems rarely have a single "right" solution. If, then, a group problem-solving strategy that is directed toward finding the "correct" solution to a problem is unreasonable, how can we characterize group problem solving?

It is our contention that group communication functions in problem-solving and decision-making situations to allow for the formulation and expression of judgment. We do not treat the expressed judgment as accurate or inaccurate; rather, we are concerned with the *adequacy* of the judgment. We consider the adequacy of a judgment to be a function of how defensible that judgment is when confronted by opposing points of view.

Consider in this light, the adequacy of a judgment must inevitably relate back to the factors taken into account in arriving at the judgment. If our problem is phrased in the form of a question, then there will be other subsidiary questions that must necessarily be answered before an attempt is made to answer the problem question. The subsidiary questions may be called issues. An issue is a question, capable of being answered in alternative ways, which is logically related to a broader question or proposition.

A problem solution may be considered relatively adequate if the relevant issues bearing on the problem have been taken into account in arriving at the solution. Issue relevancy is itself a matter of judgment. But we should be able to agree that for the problem situations described above, the answers to certain questions would considerably increase our confidence in the final judgment. For example, in the case involving alleged discrimination in housing, there are certain questions the human relations commission would like to have answers to before it decides whether or not to advise the renters to bring suit against the owner: (1) Does the owner own other apartments? (2) If yes, is there any evidence of discriminatory policies or practices in the owner's management of his other units? (3) Is there a history of complaints by the complaining renter? (4) If yes, is the complaint in question characteristic of other complaints emanating from the complaining renter? (5) What has been the owner's characteristic way of handling such complaints in the past? (6) Can the owner be persuaded not to continue with the eviction proceedings? (7) Can the renters be persuaded to interpret the owner's action as motivated by other than racial concerns? And so forth. To the extent that issues such as these, and others that might emerge from the group's deliberation, are taken into account in arriving at the judgment concerning the final disposition of the case, the decision may be considered adequate. To the extent that relevant issues bearing on the problem situation are ignored by the group, the group's decision may be considered inadequate. In the group communication process, insofar as it relates to problem solving, judgments are formulated and expressed by taking into account issues related to the problem situation. Within this perspective, then, we should consider two basic aspects of group problem-solving strategy. These aspects are: (1) problem formulation, and (2) formats for the analysis of issues.

Problem Formulation

If you have accumulated even a little experience in group problem-solving situations, you already know how difficult it is to get group members to agree on such an apparently simple matter as the specific problem they are discussing. If the events of the last decade have taught us nothing else, they have at least taught us not only that individuals frequently disagree concerning the appropriate solutions to problems of common concern, but also that individuals frequently disagree on what the problems are that confront us. The disagreements extend far beyond the point of establishing priorities among problems. We might agree that drug abuse, welfare reform, environmental concerns, inflation, and other such problems are important ones. We might also agree that our collective attentions should be directed toward these problem areas. But when groups of individuals meet for the purpose of deliberating on a given problem, agreement frequently ends. Disagreement arises concerning the nature of the problem, the way the problem should be viewed, and even what the group is attempting to accomplish by discussing this particular problem.

Group problem solving is a process of collective inquiry. The process requires cooperative and coordinated interaction wherein member resources are brought to bear upon issues related to a problem situation. Such cooperation and coordination is difficult without some basic agreement concerning the specific problem that confronts a group.

Perhaps an extended illustration of the point we are making would be helpful at this time. Our illustration grows from the work of Morris.[2] Here is a brief description of Morris's work before we return to the question of problem formulation. Morris had individuals in the United States, Canada, Norway, China, India, and Japan rate thirteen possible ways to live on a like-dislike scale. Subsequent analysis showed that in the United States and India five basic dimensions described individual preferences for ways to live. These five basic dimensions follow.

> *Factor A: Social Restraint and Self-Control.* The stress here is on responsible, conscientious, intelligent participation in human affairs. The orientation is primarily moral, with an awareness of the larger human and cosmic setting in which the individual lives and an acceptance of the restraints required by responsibility to this larger whole. The accent is on the appreciation and conservation of what man has attained rather than on the initiation of change. The antithesis of this factor is unrestrained and socially irresponsible enjoyment.
>
> *Factor B: Enjoyment and Progress in Action.* In this case, the stress is on delight in vigorous action to overcome obstacles. The emphasis is on the initiation of change rather than on the preservation of what has already been attained. The temper is one of confidence in man's powers rather than one of caution and restraint. The orientation is outward to society and to nature. The antithesis of the factor is a life focused on the development of the inner self.
>
> *Factor C: Withdrawal and Self-Sufficiency.* A rich inner life of heightened self-awareness is stressed. The self rather than society is the focus of attention. The emphasis is not on self-indulgence, however, but rather on the simplification and purification of the self to attain a high level of insight and awareness. Control over persons and things is repudiated, but not deep sympathy for all living things. The antithesis of the factor

2Charles Morris, *Varieties of Human Value* (Chicago: University of Chicago Press, 1956); idem, *Signification and Significance* (Cambridge: Mass.: The M.I.T. Press, 1964).

is merging the self with the social group for group achievement and enjoyment.

Factor D: Receptivity and Sympathetic Concern. The emphasis is on receptivity to persons and the nature. The source of inspiration comes from outside the self, and the person lives and develops in devoted responsiveness to this source. This factor is not as sharply defined as are the other factors, but a stress on responsive and devoted receptivity is clearly a mode of orientation different from that represented by any other factor.

Factor E: Self-Indulgence (or Sensuous Enjoyment). Sensuous enjoyment is stressed, whether it is found in the simple pleasures of life or in abandonment to the moment. The emphasis on social restraint and self-control characteristic of Factor A is rejected. The antithesis of the factor is responsible submission of oneself to social and cosmic purposes.[3]

Morris further reduced these five basic dimensions to three dimensions of value: detachment, dominance, and dependence. Dominance is related to Factor B. Detachment is related to Factors A and C. Dependence is related to Factors D and E. Of particular interest is Morris's analysis of relationships among these three dimensions of value and ways in which individuals adhering to these values characteristically "signify," "inquire," and talk to themselves and others.

Individuals who adhere to the detachment value tend to assign meaning to stimuli on the basis of their perception of what has happened, is happening, or will happen. When these individuals are confronted with problem situations, they adopt a form of inquiry labeled "designative." They tend to make factual statements about the matter.

Individuals who adhere to the dominance value tend to assign meaning on the basis of their perception of what should be done. When confronted with problem situations, they adopt a form of inquiry labeled "prescriptive." They tend to talk to themselves and others about courses of action, what should be done, and what ought to be the case.

Individuals who adhere to the dependence value tend to assign meaning on the basis of their perception of the relative values of things. When confronted with problem situations, they tend to adopt a form of inquiry labeled "appraisive." They talk to themselves and others about what is good and bad, what is preferred, and what is inherently more or less valuable.

Now assume that a student-faculty review committee is meeting to deliberate on the case of Robert Smith, a Master's Degree candidate who has admitted to having paid a professional "ghost writer" for writ-

[3]Reprinted from *Signification and Significance* (pp. 24–25) by Charles Morris by permission of The M.I.T. Press, Cambridge, Massachusetts. © 1964 by the M.I.T. Press.

ing the final report of his M.A. investigation. Consider the following initial statements by three members of this review committee.

Member A (designative): "Well, I guess what we need to know about this situation is what exactly happened. I mean, did Smith hire this guy to do his whole thesis, or just to help him with his writing? Did Smith actually do the whole study himself and hire this guy to help him with the writing, or what? Maybe we ought to talk to Smith to get our facts straight before we do anything about this case."

Member B (appraisive): "Now wait a minute, we haven't even decided whether Smith did anything wrong. I mean it happens all the time—ghost writing, term papers, master's theses, even doctoral dissertations. We all know that the system forces us to make certain ethical and moral compromises. I don't see that what Smith did was so bad. Seems to me we ought to look at this case first to decide whether he did anything that is worth our worrying about."

Member C (prescriptive): "We may be missing the point here. Smith has admitted to the charge his department brought against him. What we have to decide is what should be done about him. And it seem' to me that we have three alternatives. We can recommend that he bν expelled from the graduate program. We can recommend that his thesis not be approved, but that he be given an opportunity to do another thesis. Or we can recommend that his thesis be approved as is, and no disciplinary action be taken against him. But in my opinion, the purpose of this group is to recommend action."

Until this group is able to agree on how to formulate the problem confronting them, it is likely that their efforts will be disjunctive and uncoordinated. Group members will be attending to different issues.

For many years now, basic textbooks on group discussion have contended that there are essentially three types of propositions: fact, value, and policy. Propositions of fact deal with what is or is not the case, with what is true or false, or with what we may conclude to be true, given limits on our ability to discover truth in any given situation. Propositions of value deal with what is good and bad, with what moral or ethical positions should be supported or rejected by the group, or with what the consequences of adhering to particular values might be, compared with the consequences of adhering to competing values. Propositions of policy deal with what should or should not be done, with what action should be taken. This way of classifying discussion questions or problems is consistent with the research of Morris. It is also consistent with theoretical points of view in other social sciences, of which the following is an example:

> Suppose we take the term 'action.' One taxonomy divides it into 'physical actions' and 'communicative action,' and the latter in turn into 'descriptions' ('Mr. X is a Senator'), 'evaluations' ('Mr. X is a great man'), and 'prescriptions' ('Re-elect Senator X!').[4]

Any given problem area, whether it be welfare, pollution, war, pot, or potty-training, may be *approached* through designative, prescriptive, or appraisive forms of inquiry. Any given problem *may be formulated* as a question of fact, question of value, or question of policy. As long as the problem has been formulated so that group members know the kind of question they are attempting to answer, at least some of the potential sources of disjunction and disagreement may be anticipated and partially resolved.

Formats for the Analysis of Issues

That groups tend to be unsystematic in their approaches to problems is frequently lamented. It is also understandable. Frustration, confusion, and chaos are attributed to many groups. Indeed, the potential for confusion in groups is so great that analysis forms have been developed primarily to accomplish two purposes: (1) to focus group-member attention on common targets, so that member efforts are coordinated, (2) to allow the group to work through an orderly sequence of steps, so that group members know the problem-solving stages through which they have progressed, the stage they are currently in, and where they will be going next.

One of the more popular contemporary decision-making formats, the Delphi method, was developed partly as a way of avoiding the "pitfalls" of group interaction, including the following problems identified by Helmer:

> Compromise among divergent views, arrived at all too often under the undue influence of psychological factors, such as specious persuasion by the member with the greatest supposed authority or even merely the loudest voice, the unwillingness to abandon publicly expressed opinions, and the bandwagon effect of "majority opinions."[5]

The Delphi method is a way of pooling expert opinion under conditions of severely restricted interaction. Indeed, the participants in this

[4]Hans Zetterberg, *On Theory and Verification in Sociology* (New York: The Bedminister Press, 1965), p. 81.

[5]Olaf Helmer, "Analysis of the Future: The Delphi Method," (Santa Monica, California: RAND Corporation, March, 1967), p. 1.

decision-making process work independently and anonymously. The interaction takes a severely restricted form involving the filling out of questionnaires, and the feeding back of results to the individual participants. The format has been described in terms of the following steps:

1. The first questionnaire may call for a list of opinions involving experienced judgment, say a list of predictions or recommended activity.
2. On the second round each expert receives a copy of the list, and is asked to rate or evaluate each item by some criterion such as importance, probability of success, and so on.
3. The third questionnaire includes the list and the ratings, indicates the consensus, if any, and in effect asks the experts either to revise their opinions or else to specify their reasons for remaining outside the consensus.
4. The fourth questionnaire includes list ratings, the consensus and minority opinions. It provides a final chance for the revision of opinion.[6]

Emmons and Kaplan have reviewed some of the evidence bearing on the adequacy of decisions arrived at through the Delphi method.[7] They have suggested that the evidence supports the method, and have suggested ways of applying the method to decision-making situations. Of course, given the time demands of administering questionnaires, pooling data, writing feedback, revising opinions, etc., most ongoing problem-solving or decision-making groups find the Delphi method unusable. Additionally, groups consisting largely of "nonexperts" might find the Delphi method inappropriate. Nevertheless, we call it to your attention simply to illustrate an analysis format which structures interaction almost to the point where no interaction is present.

The imposition of some degree of structure on group communication is necessary for adequate problem solving. Our own research suggests that groups following systematic analysis forms are more likely to arrive at adequate judgments (solutions to industrial relations problems approximate "expert" solutions to the problems) than are groups given no systematic analysis form to follow in their discussions.[8] Let us consider briefly the three analysis forms involved in this research. You will recognize the first analysis form as the one described in Chapter 4, "Discussion: The Speech Communication Tradition." It is the form that

[6]John Pfeiffer, *New Look at Education* (Poughkeepsie, N.Y.: Odyssey Press, 1968), pp. 152–53.

[7]Jean F. Emmons and Lois M. Kaplan, "The Delphi Method and Decision-Making: A Futuristic Technique," paper presented to the International Communication Association Annual Conference, Phoenix, Arizona, 1971.

[8]Carl Larson, "Forms of Analysis and Small Group Problem-Solving," *Speech Monographs* 36 (1969): 452–55.

has guided the teaching of problem-solving group discussion since the late 1930s.

REFLECTIVE THINKING FORM

Reflective thinking, if translated into an analysis form that is reasonably comprehendible to group members, implies that the group's deliberations on a problem proceed through the following five steps:

1. What are the limits and specific nature of the problem?
2. What are the causes and consequences of the problem?
3. What things must an acceptable solution to the problem accomplish?
4. What solutions are available to us?
5. What is the best solution?

The unique feature of the reflective thinking form is found in step 3. Step 3 implies that after the group has developed an adequate understanding of the problem situation itself, their efforts are directed toward the identification of criteria. Criteria are developed according to which alternative problem solutions are compared for appropriateness. The basic assumption seems to be that if criteria are developed prior to the evaluation of problem solutions, then the appropriateness of such problem solutions might be more readily determined by comparing solutions with criteria. An implicit assumption seems to be that groups have difficulty judging the appropriateness of problem solutions unless they have developed some standards by which to evaluate their judgments.

IDEAL SOLUTION FORM

What we have called the ideal solution form requires that groups work through the following steps:

1. Are we all agreed on the nature of the problem?
2. What would be the ideal solution from the point of view of all the parties involved in the problem?
3. What conditions within the problem could be changed so that the ideal solution might be achieved?
4. Of the solutions available to us, which one best approximates the ideal solution?

The unique feature of this analysis form is that it focuses the group's attention on obstacles within the problem situation. The assumption is that if these obstacles can be overcome, or if conditions within the problem situation can be changed, then a solution might be developed that might be satisfactory to all or to most of the parties involved in the problem situation. Having developed an understanding of the problem, having determined whether or not an "ideal solution" can be identified, and having determined whether or not the parties involved might be expected to accept this solution, the group concerns itself with aspects of the problem situation that might be amenable to change. The group identifies obstacles to such change. Ways in which these obstacles might be overcome and conditions within the problem situation are focuses for group members' attention. The assumption seems to be that such a problem-solving format would result in the identification of the "best" solution from the point of view of the parties involved. If the "best" solution is impossible, given the problem conditions, then a solution that at least approximates the best solution should emerge from the discussion.

SINGLE QUESTION FORM

The single question form requires that a group work through the following steps:

1. What is the question whose answer is all the group needs to know in order to accomplish its purpose?
2. What subquestions must be answered before we can answer the single question we have formulated?
3. Do we have sufficient information to answer the subquestions confidently? (If yes, answer them. If no, continue below.)
4. What are the most reasonable answers to the subquestions?
5. Assuming that our answers to the subquestions are correct, what is the best solution to the problem?

The unique feature of the single question form is that it is oriented almost exclusively to the identification and resolution of issues. It makes necessary the clear formulation of a problem into a single question, one which presumably the group is capable of answering. That single question is analyzed in terms of the subquestions (issues) that are necessarily involved in the problem. An assumption of the single question form seems to be that issues must be resolved, however tentatively. There are many instances in which issues confronting a group cannot be resolved absolutely, or in terms of right-or-wrong answers. In these instances, the group is required to proceed with what they consider to be the most reasonable answers to these subquestions. An implicit assumption seems to be that having answered the subquestions, an adequate solution to the problem will emerge from relating the issues back to the single question the group has formulated.

Our own experiences with problem-solving groups have resulted in the personal conclusion that almost any analysis form, whether it be the rules of "brainstorming," the development of a "discussion outline," or any of the forms that we have mentioned above, is likely to result in a more adequate group decision than is produced by the groping, unrestricted group communication processes that many groups typically rely upon.[9] If you have an opportunity to experiment with these or other analysis forms now, or in other work on group communication, we think you will discover two things: (1) Group members are frequently capable of working systematically through even the most complicated problems. (2) Even following the most highly focused and orderly analysis forms, group communication is still an extremely variable, interesting, and creative phenomenon.

Having provided a brief introduction to the strategy of group problem solving, we must now impose the inevitable "contingencies" on this basic strategy. Perhaps the best way to acquaint you with these contingencies is to review some of the research that has attempted to identify and explain factors affecting the adequacy and outcomes of group problem solving.

Factors Affecting Problem-Solving Adequacy and Outcomes

What happens inside the head of an individual when he is confronted with a problem situation must be a terribly complicated set of processes. What happens when two individuals interact must be even more complicated, involving, as it does, the individual dynamics coupled with the interactional dynamics of the pair. What happens with a group of individuals involves not only the individual dynamics and the interpersonal dynamics, but also processes shaped by the properties of the group. Consequently, there are a great many factors of potential relevance to any discussion of processes related to group problem-solving adequacy and outcome. Rather than expose you to an extensive list of such factors, we have selected five factors currently receiving the empiri-

---

[9]Our uses of the concepts "analysis form" or "format for the analysis of issues" do not include planning guides such as PERT and CPM. These guides are useful for planning the implementation of a decision once the decision has been made. An excellent point of departure for exploring these guides is: Gerald M. Phillips, "PERT as a Logical Adjunct to the Discussion Process," *Journal of Communication* 15 (1965): 89–99.

cal and theoretical attention of group communication scholars. The five factors described below illustrate those things that you need to consider to understand group problem solving.

THE RISKY-SHIFT PHENOMENA

One of the more recent findings in investigations of group problem solving is that decisions made by groups are frequently riskier than decisions made by individuals.[10] That is, in situations involving some risk, group decisions are frequently riskier than the average individual judgment of the same group members. Perhaps an example would be helpful. There are about a dozen problems frequently used in exploring risky-shift phenomena. The following is one of them.

> Mr. A., an electrical engineer, is married and has one child, and has been working for a large electronics corporation since graduating from college five years ago. He is assured of a lifetime job with a modest, though adequate salary, and liberal pension benefits upon retirement. On the other hand, it is very unlikely that his salary will increase much before he retires. While attending a convention, Mr. A. is offered a job with a small, newly founded company that has a highly uncertain future. The new job would pay more to start and would offer the possibility of a share in the ownership if the company survived the competition of the larger firms.
>
> Imagine that you are advising Mr. A. Listed below are several probabilities or odds of the new company proving financially sound. Please check the lowest probability that you could consider acceptable to make it worthwhile for Mr. A. to take the new job.
>
> _____ The chances are 1 in 10 that the company will prove financially sound.
> _____ The chances are 3 in 10 that the company will prove financially sound.
> _____ The chances are 5 in 10 that the company will prove financially sound.
> _____ The chances are 7 in 10 that the company will prove financially sound.
> _____ The chances are 9 in 10 that the company will prove financially sound.

Prior to discussion, the average position checked by group members expressing individual judgments might be toward the "pretty good odds" end of the continuum. Following discussion, the group decision might be toward the "pretty slim odds" end of the continuum. This risky-shift

[10]N. Kogan and M. Wallach, "Risk Taking as a Function of the Situation, the Person and the Group," in *New Directions in Psychology*, ed. G. Mandler, P. Mussen, N. Kogan, and M. Wallach (New York: Holt, Rinehart & Winston, 1967).

does not always occur. Indeed, groups sometimes produce decisions that are more cautious than the average prediscussion individual decisions.[11] But in empirical investigations of the phenomenon risky-shift has happened much more often than not. Risky-shift, when we are talking about problems that involve some degree of risk, must be considered a factor affecting group problem-solving outcomes.

Hamilton has identified four major theoretical explanations for the risky-shift phenomenon:

1. The *diffusion of responsibility* for the decision among other group members.
2. The *exchange of information* and hence greater familiarity with the problem and the alternatives for solving it.
3. The greater *persuasiveness* or *influence* of those group members who are initially high-risk takers.
4. The social desirability of risk as a *cultural* value.[12]

The "diffusion of responsibility" explanation assumes that when a person is expressing an individual judgment he alone assumes the responsibility for the consequences of that judgment. When that same individual is involved in the process of arriving at a collective decision, however, responsibility is shared by other group members. In a sense, the group provides the individual some degree of anonymity. That is, the probability decreases that the consequences of the judgment will be linked directly to any single individual involved in the collective judgment made by the group.

The "exchange of information" explanation assumes that group members become more familiar with the alternatives after engaging in exchanges of information relevant to the problem situation. Implicit within this theoretical explanation is the assumption that the lack of familiarity with the problem situation and the alternatives results in a more conservative judgment. The underlying explanation seems to be that we are more cautious in dealing with unknown or "less-well-known" situations, and that increased familiarity results in reduced cautiousness.

The "persuasiveness of risk-takers" explanation assumes that individuals who are initially high-risk takers are also more persuasive group members. The relationship between risk taking and persuasiveness has received many explanations. We are in favor of the explanation that high-risk takers also tend to be more extroverted. Extroverted

---

[11]J. Rabow, F. Fowler, D. Bradford, M. Hoffeller, and Y. Shibuya, "The Role of Social Norms and Leadership in Risk-Taking," *Sociometry* 29 (1966): 16–27.

[12]Paul R. Hamilton, "The Effects of Risky-Shift Phenomena on Disclosure and Interaction in the Small Group Setting," unpublished paper, Illinois State University, January 6, 1972.

members probably talk more than other group members. Later in this chapter we will offer evidence that more talkative group members tend to be more influential and also tend to be evaluated more favorably by other group members.

The "cultural value" explanation assumes that when group members perceive that the problem involves some degree of risk, a valuation of caution or risk follows. Through discussion, group members learn that others have taken positions equal to or riskier than their own and may perceive themselves as no riskier than others. If, as is assumed, a cultural norm is present with respect to risk as a value, then members may shift to risk as a way of demonstrating adherence to this value.

The evidence bearing on these explanations is still indecisive. The evidence that risky-shift phenomena occur in group decision making is, however, fairly impressive. It is a phenomenon that may be expected to operate in those problem situations involving some degree of risk. As such, it as a factor to be considered in understanding group problem-solving outcomes.

CONFORMITY

If you will recall from our review of research in Chapter 2, one of the first conclusions considered well established in group communication research was that majority opinion exerts great pressures on individual attitudes and judgments. Subtle and sometimes not-so-subtle pressures are brought to bear on group members to accept majority points of view. "Excommunication," the severing of communicative bonds, exists as an implicit threat against those who deviate too far from accepted group standards. The concept of conformity to group pressure has become so commonplace that it has been a part of our popular culture for decades, forming the basic theme for movies (e.g., *Executive Suite, No Down Payment*), the lyrics of popular songs (e.g., "Pleasant Valley Sunday," "Harper Valley PTA"), and other forms of public expression. We may only assume that you are already well aware of this phenomenon.

Hoffman has reviewed experimental evidence on this point.[13] Most problem-solving groups tend to arrive at unanimous answers. About half of the time, these unanimous answers are unanimously "incorrect" or poor solutions. Members of unanimously "incorrect" groups tend to be more satisfied with their decisions than members of groups where differences of opinion existed concerning the appropriate solution. We should

---

[13]L. R. Hoffman, "Group Problem Solving," in *Advances in Experimental Social Psychology*, ed. Leonard Berkowitz (New York: Academic Press, 1965), pp. 99–132.

realize that pressures toward uniformity exist even among groups that are themselves presumably nontypical groups. The Satan Worshippers, Sigma Chi's, Hells Angels, and the Cabinet of the United States all may be quite unique in membership and formal procedures. Nevertheless, the expression of divergent viewpoints may be infrequently tolerated in each of these groups. Herein lies the relationship between pressures toward uniformity and the outcomes of problem-solving group communication. Group members may refrain from expressing divergent points of view if they have a relatively well-developed perception of the attitudes, values, and beliefs acceptable to other members of the group.

This factor is further complicated by the fact that pressures toward uniformity have rational origins. From early childhood on, we have grown accustomed to formulating and maintaining beliefs on the basis of social consensus. Many of the beliefs that we hold are held only because others share them. Our beliefs about time, speed, distance, and rate of change are based on social consensus. Certain historical and geographical beliefs are held with absolute confidence only because everyone we have encountered shares them. Indeed, many of your beliefs may be in things you have never actually experienced, yet you are confident in the socially defined truth of the situation. It is understandable, then, that individuals might question the value or validity of their own beliefs or ideas when confronted by a contradictory social consensus. The problem, of course, is that there are many instances when the validity of an individual's position is not appropriately evaluated in terms of social consensus. This is especially true when the social consensus is a narrowly defined one and is restricted to a particular group. In those instances, the adequacy of a group's solution will depend upon the extent to which divergent points of view have been considered. Thus, we are led to the consideration of another factor, one which is conceptually related to pressures toward uniformity.

EXPLOITING CONFLICT

The superiority of problem-solving groups consisting of dissimilar rather than similar types of members has been well established.[14] Mixed-sex groups and groups consisting of individuals with different personalities, differing decision-making approaches, different age groupings, dissimilar religious and political attitudes, and other heterogeneous group compositions have been found to generate more effective and/or more creative problem solutions than groups consisting of members who are

14Ibid., p. 113.

similar with respect to the above characteristics. To the extent that group members possess a comparatively wide range of experiences, beliefs, attitudes, and ideas that can be brought to bear upon particular issues, the adequacy with which issues are resolved should be increased. Hoffman has stated the point this way: "Faced with differing alternatives, none of which is acceptable to the entire group, the members may be encouraged either to search for new solutions or to integrate the alternative suggestions into a more complete and a more effective single possibility."[15]

Conflict can be either creative or disruptive. If the conflict is based primarily on different interpretations of experience, different facts, or different knowledge, then conflict can lead the group to a discovery of a better solution or a better resolution to an issue than would be possible if all group members shared essentially the same positions. Indeed, there is some evidence that when conflict is used constructively group members are more satisfied with their solutions than are members of other groups which initially agree on solutions.[16] Where conflict is based primarily on personal animosities—likes and dislikes that members have for each other—then conflict can be destructive. The key to exploiting conflict in group problem-solving situations is to keep group members' attention focused on substantive issues. If members' attentions are focused on substantive issues, then the creative use of conflict involves facilitating or encouraging the expression of divergent points of view. One of the more effective ways of facilitating the expression of divergent points of view is the effective use of developmental leadership.

DEVELOPMENTAL LEADERSHIP

Maier and Solem have demonstrated that groups in which a discussion leader is present (compared with groups in which an observer is present but does not perform leadership functions) are characterized by greater attention to and consideration of minority opinions. These researchers reported:

> The results are interpreted to mean that a discussion leader can function to up-grade group's thinking by permitting an individual with a minority opinion time for discussion. In a leaderless discussion the majority dominates and this condition releases social pressure which has an important influence on opinion. Without the right kind of leadership, therefore, a minority cannot effectively compete with the pressure of the

15Ibid., p. 117.
16N. R. F. Maier and L. R. Hoffman, "Financial Incentives and Group Decision in Motivating Change," *Journal of Social Psychology* 64 (1964): 369–78.

majority. When the minority opinion is right, and there is no protection from the leader, a distinct potential contribution is lost; when it is wrong, the minority cannot convince the majority. The leader, in giving the minority a greater voice, can up-grade the end result of a discussion without running the risk of down-grading the end product.[17]

The framework within which a discussion leader both focuses attention on issues and facilitates the expression of divergent points of view is a framework that Maier calls developmental leadership. The developmental technique is a very simple one. Its essence is that a discussion leader has analyzed a problem situation sufficiently to develop a list of subproblems within that problem situation. The discussion leader then directs the group members' attentions to these subproblems and guides the group's activities toward the solution of these subproblems. The basic requirement is preliminary analysis and advance planning on the part of the discussion leader. The technique is not greatly dissimilar from the use of the structured analysis format, which we discussed earlier in this chapter. Nor is it inconsistent with the leadership guidelines presented in Chapter 6. The main difference is that the developmental technique implies that the issues (or subproblems) are phrased in terms of the specific conditions within the problem situation. In other words, the developmental technique employs an analysis format that was developed specifically for a given problem situation.

PARTICIPATION LEVELS

A factor related to the adequacy of problem-solving deliberations is the relationship between a member's talkativeness and his influence on problem-solving outcomes. A frequent research finding on group problem solving is that more talkative group members are perceived by other members as more influential, more effective, or as "leaders" of the group.[18] In one of the early studies of this phenomenon, the researcher gave "hints" concerning a problem solution to the most talkative and the least talkative group members. Groups that contained a most talkative hint-holder generally arrived at the appropriate solution to the

---

[17]N. R. F. Maier and A. R. Solem, "The Contribution of a Discussion Leader to the Quality of Group Thinking: The Effective Use of Minority Opinions," in *Problem Solving and Creativity in Individuals and Groups,* ed. Norman R. F. Maier (Belmont, California: Brooks/Cole Publishing Co., 1970), p. 228.

[18]See, e.g., J. P. Kirscht, T. M. Lodahl, and M. Haire, "Some Factors in the Selection of Leaders by Members of Small Groups," *Journal of Abnormal and Social Psychology* 58 (1959): 406–8, as well as the research reviewed in Chapter 2, "Group Communication Research: The Speech Communication Perspective."

problem. Groups that contained the least talkative hint-holder generally rejected the solution proposed by this individual.[19]

The influence of talkativeness on problem-solving outcomes would not even be a factor for you to take into account if it were the case that more talkative group members made more helpful contributions to the discussion. Unfortunately, the relationship between talkativeness and influence seems to hold even when the more talkative members' contributions are misleading rather than helpful. Consequently, the participation levels of group members is a factor that needs to be taken into account in understanding problem-solving outcomes. If you are sensitive to this factor, you can resist the temptation to conclude that a given solution represents the group's consensus simply because it has received the consistent support of several of the most vocal members of the group.

The five factors we have just discussed by no means exhaust those which need to be considered in understanding group problem-solving outcomes. Nevertheless, they are representative of the kinds of things that can inhibit or facilitate effective group problem solving. We are all limited in our capacities to take into account a wide range of group communication phenomena, many of which occur simultaneously. The intent of this chapter was to introduce you to group problem solving. If the basic group problem-solving strategy is understood, you may contribute somewhat less to the chaos and slightly more to problem-solving adequacy. If you can consider even a few of the factors that are associated with problem-solving adequacy, your performance in problem-solving groups should improve.

SUMMARY

1. Small-group decision making and problem solving permeates our lives and is one of the basic processes upon which our society relies.

2. Unfortunately, experience alone tends not to be the best teacher—if group communication in this area is to be improved we must bolster our experience with insight into the processes operating.

3. The problems confronting groups rarely have "correct" solutions. Rather, the judgments expressed in group problem solving should be viewed as adequate or inadequate according to how defensible a particular judgment is when confronted by opposing points of view.

4. Any given problem may be approached through these forms of in-

---

[19]H. W. Riecken, "The Effect of Talkativeness on Ability to Influence Group Solutions of Problems," *Sociometry* 21 (1958): 309–21.

quiry: designative (making factual statements about the matter), prescriptive (talking about courses of action and what ought to be the case), or appraisive (talking about what is good and bad, what is preferred).

5. Any given problem may be formulated as a question of fact, value, or policy. It is important that group members know the kind of question they are attempting to answer.

6. Research suggests that groups following systematic analysis forms are more likely to arrive at adequate judgments than groups not following such systems.

A. The reflective thinking form stresses that a group should develop standards for evaluating the appropriateness of their problem solutions.

B. The ideal solution form focuses the group's attention on the obstacles within the problem situation.

C. The single question form, which necessitates the formulation of a problem into a single question, is oriented almost exclusively to the identification and resolution of issues.

7. In order to understand group problem solving several factors that affect adequacy and outcomes need to be considered:

A. Where risk is involved, group decisions are likely to be riskier than decisions made by individual members of the group.

B. Group members may refrain from expressing divergent points of view because of the inherent pressures within a group to conform.

C. Problem-solving groups possessing members with a comparatively wide range of experiences, beliefs, and attitudes and ideas usually are superior to groups with similar types of members. The resultant conflict can be exploited to advantage if members' attention is focused on substantive issues rather than on personal animosities.

D. Groups with discussion leaders are characterized by greater attention to the issues and by greater attention to minority opinions.

E. The relationship between a member's talkativeness or participation level and his influence is related to solution adequacy—talkative members can of course make both helpful and misleading contributions.

experiencing group communication

OBJECTIVES

After studying this chapter, you should be able to:

Understand the experiential or laboratory approach to group communication.

Examine the basic characteristics and assumptions of the laboratory approach in everyday contexts as opposed to those dimensions of behavior in a laboratory training group.

Recognize the influence the laboratory approach has had on teaching and scholarship in group communication.

Evaluate the consequences of participating in laboratory group experience.

Reach a personal decision as to whether you wish to understand or participate in a laboratory experience.

Fundamental to teaching and scholarship in group communication is the notion that group communication processes, in order to be understood, should be experienced. For almost half a century, teachers of group discussion, and more recently teachers of group dynamics and group process, have invented an amazing array of experiences, exercises, and training designs, all for the sake of helping individuals understand what is happening in groups and within themselves when they are in groups.

These experiences range from the conventional to the bizarre, from the sedate to the mind-boggling, from the everyday to the once-in-a-lifetime.

If the conduct of group communication experiences varies widely, depending upon the philosophy of the teacher or "trainer," the reactions of participants in these experiences vary even more widely. In a single session we have observed participant reactions ranging from the extreme of one individual's declaration that her entire life has been changed by the experience she had just gone through to the other extreme of an individual's dramatic departure from the room after having written "bull shit" in letters as large as the blackboard would allow. In our experience as T-group trainers, we have observed a strange but apparently regular concurrence of phenomena: (1) individuals frequently respond intensely, whether positively or negatively, to group experiences; (2) these same individuals frequently have great difficulty explaining or interpreting the experiences that served as the impetus for these responses. We have occasionally overheard or been a party to dialogues that ran something like the following: "What a fantastic experience. I learned more about myself than I thought was possible. People in the group were beautiful, caring people. We grew, learned, discovered. It was wonderful." "Well, tell me what happened in this group." "Well . . . I'm not really sure."

Experiential approaches to group communication are difficult to describe precisely because they are experiential in nature. Nevertheless, it is important that we attempt to acquaint you with some of the concepts associated with the experiential approach to group communication, since these concepts have influenced scholarship and teaching in group communication.

The Laboratory Approach: A Brief History

The laboratory approach is a generic term which encompasses "T-group" (T for training), "Sensitivity training," "Encounter groups," and the great variety of offshoots thereof. The principles underlying the laboratory approach had their origin in 1946, on a college campus in Connecticut.[1] A summer workshop was held involving teachers, social workers, and a variety of other participants who met for the purpose of discussing ways in which local leaders might be developed to aid in securing understanding of and compliance with the Fair Employment Practices Act.

---

[1]For a detailed discussion of the history of T-groups, see Kenneth D. Benne, "History of the T-Group in the Laboratory Setting," in *T-Group Theory and Laboratory Method*, ed. Leland P. Bradford, Jack R. Gibb, and Kenneth Benne (New York: Wiley, 1964).

The participants met in small discussion groups and worked on problems they had encountered in the communities from which they had come. The workshop was staffed by social scientists. These social scientists held evening meetings in which they discussed their observations of the processes that characterized the daily meetings of the workshop participants. The social scientists analyzed and interpreted leadership, member behavior, and group phenomena.

Some of the workshop participants began attending these evening meetings. For the participants, attending a meeting wherein one's behavior was openly discussed, in terms of how others perceived the behavior and its consequences, was apparently a very involving and enlightening experience. Before long, all of the workshop participants were attending these evening meetings. The participants joined in the effort to analyze and interpret the processes that were occurring in the daily discussion groups. "To the training staff it seemed that a potentially powerful medium and process of re-education had been, somewhat inadvertently, hit upon. Group members, if they were confronted more or less objectively with data concerning their own behavior and its effects, and if they came to participate nondefensively in thinking about these data, might achieve highly meaningful learnings about themselves, about the responses of others to them, and about group behavior and group development in general."[2]

The effects of this experience were apparently stimulating and exciting, both to the participants and to the staff. Subsequently, some of the staff began planning ways in which similar learning situations could be provided for other participants. This planning led to the establishment of the National Training Laboratory for Group Development (NTL), which sponsored a formal training program the following summer, 1947, in Bethel, Maine. A basic element in this training program was a small group in which an observer made his observations available for analysis by the group and in which the group leader ("trainer") assisted the group in analyzing the observations and in discussing observations made by the leader and group members. This kind of group eventually became known as a T-group and provided the basic format from which has sprung many variations of group-oriented laboratory training.

From such inauspicious beginnings came an educational innovation that is, perhaps, one of the more significant of this century. At the very least, it has established itself as a part of the popular culture, finding its way into the literature, the entertainment media, and the everyday language of increasing numbers of people. Our understanding of this

[2]Benne, History of the T-Group," p. 83.

phenomenon might be enhanced by considering three interrelated observations.

1. At the very core of the laboratory approach is the concept of "feedback." It has been argued that within an individual's complex system of beliefs, among the more primitive and early developed beliefs are those that have to do with identity or self.[3] Our beliefs about self occupy a central position in our system of beliefs. They are therefore important determinants of the nature, content, and organization of many other beliefs in the belief system. Beliefs about self originate in communicative exchanges with others. Consensual validation for our beliefs about self are obtained by noting or observing the responses of others to us. It is understandable, then, that an educational method that encourages "feedback," or that allows us to obtain information about how others view us, proves to be, for most people, an extremely involving experience. Of course, the observation that feedback can be an extremely involving experience leads quite naturally to another observation: we apparently have difficulty obtaining feedback from others, especially the kind of feedback that we may confidently assume reflects honest and authentic responses of others to us.

2. In order to understand the early success and growth of laboratory approaches to group communication, one must attend to the fact that things have changed over the last quarter of a century. In the late forties, through the fifties, and into the sixties, there emerged and solidified a certain conventional characterization of the American culture. It was materialistic. Success was obtained through the accumulation of power, status, and the possession of material objects. Individuals were seen as occupying roles, and as motivated to behave in ways consistent with those roles, with the emphasis being on the appropriateness of the behavior for the role. Individual aspirations were seen as antithetical or subservient to the goals of institutions. Interpersonal relationships were seen as consisting largely of facade, ritual. A major portion of entertainment fare consisted of offerings such as *The Man in the Grey Flannel Suit, Executive Suite, No Down Payment, The Young Philadelphians, View From the Terrace,* and an uninterrupted stream of both fictional and nonfictional works that reflected an image of man as trapped by institutions, social rituals, and roles, and as sacrificing personal fulfillment in order to conform to the expectations of others. To a certain extent, this picture of man had been painted before and continues to be painted at present. It seems to us, however, that this characterization of the American experience was intensified in the years that surrounded

[3]Milton Rokeach, *Beliefs, Attitudes, and Values* (San Francisco: Jossey-Bass, 1968).

the emergence and growth of the "human relations" movement with its associated laboratory approaches to learning. It was partially this climate that provided such a dramatic contrast between the kinds of experiences individuals could obtain in T-groups and the kinds of interpersonal experiences individuals had become accustomed to in their daily routine. To the extent that this picture of American life continues to be accurate (if, indeed, it ever was accurate), then the laboratory approach will probably remain with us for quite some time. At any rate, it is un-important for our present purposes whether you agree with the above characterization of American life. If you are to understand the laboratory approach, however, you should know that a picture of contemporary society somewhat similar to the one alluded to above continues to be held by many proponents of the laboratory approach:

> Why all of the current interest in the intensive group encounter? For one thing it appears to be a significant part of the cultural attempt to meet the isolation of contemporary life. I am not fond of the often faddish elements in it, but in general the small group experience fulfills a need. From a social point of view, I believe we are sufficiently affluent that our physical needs are met, and now what would we most like to have? We would like to be free from the alienation that is so much a part of urban life, so much a part of our life in general. We would like somehow to find ourselves in real contact with other persons, and I believe this desire, without question, is one of the elements that gives much of the magnetism to the intensive group experience. The person who has come close to experiencing a real I-Thou relationship in a group is no longer an isolated individual.[4]

3. Our third comment further establishes the perspective from which the laboratory approach may be viewed. The original focus of T-groups was on group processes and on member behavior that related to group processes. The kinds of conceptual issues around which T-group training was oriented were not unlike the conceptual issues treated in this book: difficulties encountered by groups in using member re-sources to solve problems; problems experienced by groups in getting organized; how to assist group members in observing, diagnosing, and understanding group processes; the leadership role, and member re-sponses to leadership attempts by a formal leader or by other members of the group; the roles played by group members, and consequences of member behavior, both in terms of its impact on group process and on the interpersonal perceptions that emerge from interaction; etc. Under-lying the early focus of T-group training were three general training

[4]Carl Rogers, in the foreword to *New Perspectives on Encounter Groups*, ed. Lawrence N. Solomon and Betty Berzon (San Francisco: Jossey-Bass, 1972).

goals :(1) developing diagnostic and behavioral skills that the participant could employ in his "back-home" setting, (2) developing conceptual frameworks through which the participant could understand the nature of groups and the behavior of individuals in groups, and (3) providing relatively intense and involving situations through which the participants learn on the emotional as well as the conceptual level. Given these general objectives, and the comparative novelty of the laboratory approach itself, it was inevitable that divergent points of view would develop concerning what kinds of learning experiences to provide for participants, the extent to which the learning should be conceptually or emotionally based, whether to orient the training toward the personal growth and development of the participant, or whether to emphasize skill development designed to improve the effectiveness of the individuals' back-on-the-job performance. Over the years, there seems to have developed two major trends toward laboratory training. These trends are described by Lakin as interactional awareness and expanded experiencing.[5]

Of the two, the "interactional awareness" approach has remained more consistent with the original focus of T-groups. Part of Lakin's description of this approach includes the following:

> The group processes of training constitute the initial focus for learnings in this trend. The conceptual language is mainly that of group dynamics and social interaction. The inner experiences of individuals are relevant as they bear upon the group process, and individual learnings are interpersonal as well as personal. Overall interpersonal effectiveness and the capacity to facilitate change as needed are the major goals. Success as a group member is reflected in becoming a positive force in the context of the microcommunity. The important learnings in such training groups appear to be skills in understanding and coping with interactional processes, learning how to give help to other members, how to facilitate a group's efforts toward its goals, how to increase everyone's participation, and how to develop better communication among the members of the group and between groups. When adherents of this trend use terms such as insight, awareness, diagnosis, growth, etc., the referent is the interpersonal self. The interpersonal rather than the intrapsychic realm is the primary area of development, improvement, and change.[6]

The "expanded experiencing" approach emphasizes intense personal-emotional encounters oriented toward personal growth.[7] The Esalen

---

[5]Martin Lakin, *Interpersonal Encounter: Theory and Practice in Sensitivity Training* (New York: McGraw-Hill, 1972), p. 20.

[6]Ibid., p. 21. Reprinted by permission from McGraw-Hill Book Company.

[7]See, e.g., Carl Rogers, *On Encounter Groups* (New York: Harper and Row, 1970); William C. Schutz, *Joy* (New York: Grove Press, 1967).

Institute groups, the encounter groups popularized by Carl Rogers, and the many offshoots of encounter group methods all illustrate this approach. Emphasis is placed on overcoming inhibitions, developing spontaneity, creativity, and emotional expressiveness and responsiveness, and reawakening sensory awareness. Participants in groups oriented toward an expanded experiencing may become involved in nonverbal exercises, body movement exercises, physical contact, meditation, "induced aggression," sessions or total training programs conducted in the nude, or any of a number of other experiences designed to free the inner self, expand consciousness, or further the creative potential of participants. A part of Lakin's description of this approach includes the following:

> Trainers in this trend used training group processes to explore individual personality factors which are reflected in them rather than to study interpersonal processes per se. They employed the terminology of clinical psychology and psychotherapy. Group processes are thus likely to be interpreted as shared collusive defenses, or more likely, to be altogether disregarded in favor of attention to individual dynamics or intrapersonal defenses. Trainers in this stream hold that training and psychotherapy share the objectives of ego strengthening, deeper experiencing, and an improved self-image. Training and therapy also involve the development of insight for correction of personal problems and provide opportunities for reality testing in this view. In general, adherents of this trend see the trainer as a rather special kind of guide who elicits self-disclosure frequently by modeling it himself. The aim of the trend was also to help the participant overcome various personal deficiencies attributed to inhibitions or stilted expressiveness. This approach sees in the training group a means of providing "therapy for normals" on the assumption that presumably effective and competent persons are neither as effective nor as competent as they appear to be, especially in the social emotional aspects of living. To achieve the needed change toward personal improvement, this trend prescribes high emotional involvement and intense interpersonal encounters in the group setting.[8]

The distinctions between these two approaches to laboratory training are not absolute. Within each general approach there is still a great variety of methods, philosophies, and values adhered to by the practitioners of the approaches. Nevertheless, the distinction made by Lakin, on a general level, seem appropriate. Throughout the remainder of this chapter, our use of the term "laboratory approach" will refer predominantly to the interactional awareness orientation. This is the approach that is most consistent with the focus of this book, that focus being group communication processes.

    [8]Lakin, *Interpersonal Encounter*, pp. 22–23. Reprinted by permission from McGraw-Hill Book Company.

Assumptions of the Laboratory Approach

The laboratory approach has five essential characteristics: (1) An experience-oriented learning situation. Participants learn by observing and analyzing problems confronting the group in the "here-and-now." Ordinarily, a minimum degree of initial structure is provided for the group members. As the group develops its own structure, identifies its learning objectives, or decides on ways in which it might accomplish certain objectives, the trainer and participants attempt to uncover and understand factors that operate at the group or individual level and assist or hinder the group in its progress. The focus is on the "here-and-now" in the sense that the attention of the members is directed toward problems and processes that emerge during the group experience itself. (2) A feedback system. Observations, perceptions, and reactions of group members are made available to other members. These become data against which members may compare their own understanding of significant events and processes, as well as the effects of their own behavior on other group members. (3) An opportunity to plan, employ, and evaluate new behavior in an atmosphere conducive to such experimentation. Members are encouraged to go beyond their characteristic modes of behavior to develop a wider range of behavioral skills. (4) An atmosphere of emotional support for the learner. If group members are to experiment with new behaviors, and if relatively explicit feedback is to occur, then such experiences must be accompanied by emotional and psychological support for the learner. The trainer and the group itself, since the experience is a shared one, provide the personal support that is frequently necessary whenever individuals enter strange or unusual areas. (5) A program of supplementary learning experiences. The processes that freely occur within the laboratory group are frequently supplemented by structured training experiences usually designed to provide conceptual insight into group or interpersonal processes.

These essential features of the laboratory approach rest upon a number of assumptions: (1) The participants are themselves responsible for their own learning. The course of events in the group is shaped by the participants. The value of the group as a learning vehicle is determined by the extent to which the participants take advantage of the opportunities that are provided for acquiring insights into themselves and the group process. The participants are responsible to each other, and that responsibility cannot be shifted to persons or conditions outside of the group or to the training staff. (2) Experience in groups, in and of itself, is not sufficient to provide for valid learning. If experience in groups were sufficient, we would all be more effectively functioning group members than we seem to be. The T-group provides a more intensive experience than that which we obtain from other, nonlaboratory groups. During the course of a typical T-group, the members are exposed, in a brief but highly intensified form, to a full range of phenomena. From the chaotic, confusing, and frequently uncertain birth of a group to its death and dissolution, members encounter magnified versions of group and interpersonal processes that are characteristic of a variety of nonlaboratory groups. (3) Learning is facilitated when individuals establish authentic relationships with others. If individuals are direct with each other, if feelings are expressed rather than inhibited, if responses and observations are related honestly, then the learning that occurs is more likely to be valid. (4) Feelings are real data. If raised to an explicit level, and if obtained from all or a majority of the group members, feelings and observations provide the data base from which learning can proceed. (5) Learning can be facilitated by examining the basic values from which an individual operates. As the individual examines his basic values in terms of new concepts and new ideas, he is able to develop a greater sense of personal worth, or self-confidence, and deeper and more constructive interpersonal relationships with others.

The extent to which these assumptions are valid is open to contention. An indirect argument in favor of their validity is the dramatic growth in popularity of laboratory training programs over the last two decades. In the interests of fairness, it should be noted that the same argument might reasonably have been advanced at times to support the validity of the assumptions underlying such programs as the Dale Carnegie courses, military academies, psychoanalysis, transcendental meditation, and the U.S. Marine Corps. We would be naive to suggest that there are ultimate, lasting, and universal truths awaiting you somewhere in a T-group. On the other hand, there may be some small, perhaps temporary, and somewhat personal truths that can emerge from laboratory training. Our own position on the matter is that there is some learning which apparently occurs in laboratory group experiences that is difficult, if not impossible, to obtain elsewhere. The nature of the experience, and the learning that might result from it, may be further explicated if we examine the values and behavioral prescriptions that have become associated with the laboratory approach.

Implicit Values
in the Laboratory Approach

We have already indicated that most proponents of the laboratory approach subscribe to the notion that man and society are engaged in a life of continuous role playing. Most of the roles are allegedly contrived, and most of the behavior associated with these roles is superficial. Much of human interchange is seen as facade meeting facade, with little opportunity for "authentic" encounters. Given this image of man in society, it is perhaps natural and inevitable that proponents of the laboratory approach would emphasize several implications of these assumptions: (1) many human relationships are not as they should be; (2) we know how they should be.

In their attempts to improve the character of human relationships, proponents of the laboratory approach have been criticized for imposing, unobtrusively but deliberately, a set of quite personal values on others. The criticism proceeds with the assertion that in their attempt to provide a mechanism through which individuals can break from the conformity that so characterizes contemporary American life, proponents of the laboratory approach have inadvertently instituted a different type of conformity. The arguments go full circle, and arrive at the "same to you, buddy" stage, when one proponent answers a critic by saying: "I cannot resist the comment that any conformity induced by encounter groups is as nothing compared to the conformity absolutely demanded by graduate departments of psychology!"[9]

It would be unreasonable for us to ignore the criticisms which state that the laboratory approach is, in essence, a value-based strategy for providing learning experiences. This is probably true, to at least some extent, of all training, education, and other forms of indoctrination. Admitting that implicit values are operating in the laboratory approach allows us to shift our attention to the nature of these values, or at least to the areas of human interaction in which these values operate. Such a shift in focus is more profitable to your understanding of the laboratory approach and to any personal decision you might make with respect to participating in sensitivity training or T-groups. Since there is considerable variety in types of laboratory group experiences, in the structure of these experiences, and in trainer orientations toward such experiences, we must approach the description of implicit values in the laboratory approach somewhat cautiously. We must first provide a conceptual framework that may facilitate subsequent identification of implicit values. Let us shift our attention for awhile to the following conceptual framework.

Are you warm enough right now? That is, is the temperature in the room or the place where you are reading this book comfortable? Is it a little too warm, or a little too cold? Odds are that for most of the people reading this book at this very moment the temperature is a comfortable one. Indeed, there is a range of temperatures across which

[9]Rogers, *New Perspectives on Encounter Groups*, p. ix.

you will remain comfortable; in fact, you will probably not even attend to or notice the temperature as long as it remains within this "comfort" range. You will be oblivious to or at least inattentive to "temperature" as long as you remain indoors because indoor temperatures are adjusted to our comfort levels. When the temperature exceeds your comfort range, either at the top or at the bottom of the scale, you will notice it. This is true of many physical stimuli, such as temperature, lighting, humidity, etc.

Now consider a somewhat different class of stimuli, including both physical and social dimensions. Consider the distance that is maintained between two individuals when they are interacting. Most of the time that you are talking to other individuals you are not conscious of or not attending to the physical distance between you and the other. You are comfortable within a range of physical distances. But if another person, while you are talking with him, approaches you to the point that his face is four inches away from yours, your comfort range will probably have been violated and you will attend to or notice the physical distance between you and the other. In our culture, and in most social contexts within it, we are accustomed to maintaining certain physical distances between conversants. As long as two people do not stand too close to each other or too distant from each other when they are talking, odds are that neither will notice or attend to the physical distance separating them. This, and other interesting combinations of physical and social stimuli, provide the substance for theory and research in the area that has become identified as "nonverbal communication."[10]

Finally, let us shift our attention to a class of stimuli that are essentially social. Consider, for example, intimacy and disclosure. If you interact with another person, especially if that interaction proceeds beyond a first, casual meeting, then the interaction may be characterized by varying degrees of disclosure. You may disclose certain feelings, values, past experiences, future hopes or desires, and other "personal" things to the person with whom you are interacting. The other person may engage in similar disclosures. Much of the time these disclosures occur as a natural consequence of the developing relationship. Sometimes the disclosures provide the impetus for a deepening of the relationship or a change in its nature. In most of your everyday interaction with others, you probably do not attend to the disclosures that are made. Your relationships with others probably remain comfortable for you across a range of degrees of disclosure or intimacy. If, however, your interaction with another over a period of time has resulted in the other's disclosing

---

[10]See, e.g., Mark L. Knapp, *Nonverbal Communication in Human Interaction* (New York: Holt, Rinehart & Winston, 1972).

nothing in terms of his personal values, sentiments, past experiences, future hopes and desires, etc., then you will notice or attend to this fact. Similarly, if you encounter an individual who immediately discloses rather personal information that is usually reserved for more intimate friends and associates, then you will notice or attend to this fact. Most of us are comfortable with each other so long as the degree of intimacy or disclosure in the relationship does not exceed that which we consider appropriate, given the length of acquaintance with the other and the context in which the interaction occurs.

Almost any kind of behavior varies in degree or in intensity. Manipulation, control or regulation, display of affection, rejection, and other forms of behavior we experience and exhibit in degrees. We are all accustomed to operating within certain tolerance limits or comfort levels with respect to the behavior we exhibit and the behavior that others exhibit and we respond to. If the behavior is within our comfort level, we tend not to attach any particular significance to it. When the behavior exceeds our comfort level, we attend to the nature of that behavior and may attach particular significance to it.

It is our belief that group processes and interpersonal behavior in T-groups are "out of the ordinary" in a number of dimensions. This is so by design because of the way the group experience is planned or structured, because of the way the trainer behaves, and because of the social science and humanistic concepts that pervade the training experience. The implicit values underlying the laboratory approach increase the probability of certain types of behavior occurring in training groups. More generally, there are certain dimensions of behavior in training groups which are sufficiently different from the nature of behavior in everyday contexts that we would notice or attend to these dimensions of behavior if we were participants in a training group. Values are extremely difficult to describe. But the implicit values underlying the laboratory approach are themselves related to certain dimensions of behavior that characterize laboratory groups. These dimensions of behavior have been called "central norm areas" by Gibb, and they represent dimensions of behavior in laboratory groups in which implicit values are likely to be operating. In fairness to Gibb, we should note that he simply describes the dimensions of behavior as "central norm areas that concern groups as they consciously attend to their own processes." We would add that these are dimensions of behavior in which implicit values are likely to be operating. Gibb describes the central norm areas as follows:

> *Risk.* The group develops more or less consistent ways of limiting risk, handling fears, testing level of risk, punishing or rewarding risk takers,

or handling those who either expose too much or fail to share in what are seen as the common dangers.

Trust. The group develops more or less stable trust levels. It develops norms about communicating trust, handling members who deviate from trust boundaries, viewing suspicions about motivations of trainers and other members, influencing what is said about the group outside the group, and building trust.

Nonconformity. The group develops ways of handling members who deviate in attitude or behavior, of expressing differential tolerance for special areas of conformity and nonconformity, and of communicating rewards and punishments both for conformity and for nonconformity.

Membership. Norms emerge about the privileges of membership, the ways of attaining membership, the degrees and levels of membership, the importance of commitment, and the expression of acceptance, affection, or approval.

Rejection. More or less consistent patterns arise in the manner of expressing rejection, ways of camouflaging rejection or disapproval, what rejectees may do, and what kinds of behavior will elicit rejection.

Feedback. In working through the data processing concerns, groups learn ways of giving feedback, receiving feedback, determining limits of feedback, determining who can give such data to whom, ignoring demands for feedback, and acceptable ways of reacting to such data.

Consensus. Norms arise as to what is meant by full or partial agreement, whether silence means assent, dissent, or indecision, how much in agreement a person must feel in order to say he agrees, how decisions are made, how decisions are ignored, and how consensus is tested.

Process. Groups develop more or less consistent habits about what kinds of process to look at, ways of looking at process, how it is integrated into action, how often it is looked at, and who is allowed to make process interventions under what conditions.

Diagnosis. Habits develop around how diagnosis is integrated into action, how much moralizing or evaluation is allowed, how often and under what conditions diagnoses are made, and how diagnosticians are given approval or disapproval.

Feeling-perception. Groups develop strong standards about whether feelings should be admitted as data, how often and by whom feelings and perceptions may be expressed, what kinds of feelings and perceptions are admissible in verbal interaction and what kinds admissible only as nonverbal data, and how significant such data are in making what kinds of decisions.

Goal determination. In working through goal-formation concerns, groups develop norms about how goals are formulated, what bearing goals have upon subsequent activity, what is done about goal diversity and incompatibility, and how explicit goals must be in order to create movement.

Reward-punishment. Norms emerge around how punishments and rewards are administered, what kinds of punishments and rewards are appropriate in the group, who can give what kinds of approval or disapproval, and how members should react to differential treatment.

Learning-growth. Particularly significant in the T-Group, but also present in action groups, are norms about how we learn, what things are seen as evidence of growth, what are acceptable ways of initiating and reacting to change, what effects conflict and exposure have in learning, from whom members are willing to learn, and how members who learn or do not learn are handled.

Provisional try. Consistent patterns emerge concerning how experimentation is carried on by individuals or by the group as a whole, to what degree decisions of the group are provisional or immutable, how formal and deliberate experimentation may be, how to punish and reward innovators, and in what areas of group life provisional behavior is sanctioned.

Work. Consistent ideas and behavior emerge around the nature of work and play, how work is avoided or accomplished, what constitutes efficiency and how important it is, and what kinds of activities are treated as productive or nonproductive.

Conflict. In resolving control concerns, groups soon meet conflict and develop characteristic ways of determining how to handle it, how to produce what kinds of conflict, how to integrate it into work and creativity or how to avoid and repress it, and how to live with different reactions to conflict among members of the group.

Permissiveness. Norms emerge about how to give or refuse permission or sanction for what kinds of behavior or attitudes, how to handle variable reactions to existing boundaries, how to communicate the permissiveness that does exist, and how to allow and to live with freedoms that emerge.

Boundaries. Groups develop boundaries of various kinds and develop norms about how boundaries arise, how they are violated, how permeable they are, how they are changed, how they are tested, and who is allowed to violate them under what conditions.

Resources. Norms arise regarding the use of people resources in the group—who are permitted to serve as resources or to give information about what; how emergent experts are ignored or used; how much information of what kind a person is allowed to give often; and what kinds of resource information are seen as special or professional.

Organization. Groups learn ways of organizing for action, what kinds of leadership roles are needed from whom, what kinds of organization will be tolerated, how organization can be changed, and how permanent or stable organization must be for what purposes.[11]

A Personal Decision

To be understood, the laboratory experience must be experienced. Whether or not you want to understand it or wish to experience it involves a personal decision. The approach embodies a potentially powerful individual learning experience, so seeking and participating in the experience is not a decision that should be made lightly. It is not for

[11] Jack R. Gibb, "Climate for Trust Formation," in *T-Group Theory and Laboratory Method*, ed. Leland P. Bradford, Jack R. Gibb, and Kenneth Benne (New York: Wiley, 1964), pp. 306–8. Reprinted by permission from John Wiley & Sons, Inc.

everyone. Nor, in our judgment, does everyone need it. Perhaps a reasonable base for assessing the value of the experience itself is the considerable amount of research that has been done in an attempt to more systematically describe the consequences of participating in laboratory group experience. The research is far from conclusive, but four tentative generalizations from empirical findings have been suggested by Seashore.[12] First, participants are likely to improve their interpersonal skills. Second, improvement, as judged by a number of studies, characterizes approximately two-thirds of the participants. Third, many participants, in anecdotal reports, claim to have undergone extremely significant changes with respect to their lives and their relationships with others. Fourth, serious stress and mental disturbance during training are extremely rare and seem to occur almost exclusively in participants who have a prior history of such disturbances.

An important aspect of the personal decision to participate in a laboratory group experience involves the question of who is conducting the experience. Before participating in a T-group, you should satisfy yourself that the individual conducting the T-group has had specific formal training in the laboratory approach. Investigate the qualifications of the training staff.

The laboratory approach continues to be one of the most exciting educational innovations of this century. In a sense, it is still in the exploratory stages of development. It has influenced and will undoubtedly continue to influence teaching and scholarship in group communication. For this reason, if for no other, individuals interested in group communication phenomena can profit from an understanding of the laboratory approach.

SUMMARY

1. Group communication processes, in odrer to be understood, should be experienced. One way to gain such experience is through the laboratory approach, a generic term which encompasses "T-groups," "sensitivity training," and "encounter groups."

2. The laboratory approach, perhaps among the more significant educational innovations of this century, is a learning situation designed to provide training in group process and communication.

3. At the core of the laboratory approach is the concept of "feedback"

---

[12]Charles Seashore, "What is Sensitivity Training," in *Sensitivity Training and the Laboratory Approach*, ed. Robert T. Golembiewski and Arthur Blumberg (Itasca, Illinois: F. E. Peacock, 1970).

which allows us to obtain information about how others view us—we apparently have difficulty obtaining honest and authentic feedback from others in everyday encounters.

4. One reason for current interest in the laboratory approach is the cultural attempt to meet the isolation of contemporary life.

5. Since its beginnings in the 1940s, two major trends toward laboratory learning have developed: (1) the "interactional awareness" approach which focuses on training for effective group process or interpersonal communication (the interpersonal realm); (2) the "expanded experience" approach which emphasizes intense personal-emotional encounters and is oriented toward personal growth (the intrapersonal realm).

6. The five essential characteristics of the laboratory approach are: (1) an experience-oriented learning situation focused on the "here-and-now"; (2) a feedback system; (3) an opportunity to plan, employ, and evaluate new behavior; (4) an atmosphere of emotional support for the learner; (5) a program of supplementary structured learning experiences.

7. The laboratory approach has several basic assumptions: (1) participants are themselves responsible for their own learning (as opposed to the staff or others outside the group); (2) experience in groups, in and of itself, is not sufficient to provide for valid learning (if it were we would all be more effective group participants than we are); (3) learning is facilitated when individuals establish authentic relationships with others; (4) feelings are real data; (5) learning can be facilitated by examining the basic values from which an individual operates.

8. Some learning apparently occurs in laboratory group experiences that is difficult, if not impossible, to obtain elsewhere.

9. Implicit values do underlie the laboratory approach; these are related to certain dimensions of behavior that characterize laboratory groups and are "out of the ordinary." Gibb offers twenty central norm areas in which implicit values are likely to be operating.

10. The laboratory approach is a potentially powerful individual learning experience, and the decision to participate in it should not be made lightly. It is useful to be aware of four tentative generalizations from empirical findings as you make such a decision:

A. Participants are likely to improve their interpersonal skills.

B. Improvement characterizes about two-thirds of the participants.

C. Many participants claim to have undergone extremely significant changes with respect to their lives and their relationships with others.

D. Serious stress and mental disturbance during training are extremely rare, and they seem to occur almost exclusively in participants who have a prior history of such disturbances.

11. It is important to investigate the qualifications of the training staff before you participate in a laboratory experience.

12. The laboratory approach continues to influence teaching and scholarship in group communication.

index